Easy Low Carb Diabetic Cookbooks for Beginners

2500+ Days of Mouthwatering and Healthy Low Sugar Recipes Suitable for Pre-Diabetic, Newly Diagnosed Type 2 Diabetes | Simple & Quick Meal Plan

Emily Bottom

Table of Content

8.3. Dinner..38

8.4. Snack..51

8.5. Desserts and Cakes

Chapter 9
Meal Plan and Index

INTRODUCTION

I'm Emily. I'd like to share a story with you that deeply moved both me and my grandmother Grace in many ways. Grandma Grace has always held a place in my heart. Growing up with her, I have memories of my childhood. Her clever jokes and captivating stories never failed to bring a smile to my face. Grandma is a strong-willed woman. Nobody can challenge her resolve—not me until a few years ago! I recall how only grandpa had the knack for soothing her temper with a glance, an act that brought peace to our household amidst all my pranks. Oh well, hindsight is 20/20! He could have stepped in sooner to calm her down. Grandpa's strength was never about timing.

Everything changed when he left us too soon. After Grandpa's passing, Grandma Grace's life was turned upside down. She became withdrawn, seeking solace in food to fill the emptiness his departure left. Her health began to decline, yet despite me becoming the closest person to her, she dismissed every piece of advice I offered. It was in trying to lighten her spirits that I discovered her sanctuary in poetry, a means to articulate her inner turmoil with words rich in emotion, pain, and hope. Yet, life did not cease to present us with new challenges. When the diagnosis of type 2 diabetes came, our world was shaken. Initially, Grandma resisted the changes needed for her health. However, the prospect of losing her beloved poetry due to visual impairment and decreased hand sensitivity caused by diabetes motivated her to declare, "I want to change." This marked a turning point for us, a brave step towards a

new chapter of health and hope. I delved into studying everything about diabetes, consulting books and experts, in search of a way to help my grandma manage her condition. My determination began to yield results. I encouraged Grandma Grace to alter her diet. Together, we started preparing healthy and delicious meals. I got her to engage in more physical activity, even if it was just short walks. Our daily routine evolved into a health journey, and Grandma Grace began to experience its benefits. Over time, she lost weight and regained her fitness. Her health stabilized, and she returned to writing poems with renewed vigor. It was as if diabetes no longer dictated her life. I asked her, "Grandma, why did you decide to change your life only when you could no longer write?" She replied, "When I write, my dear, it's as if I'm meeting your grandpa again." Then she added, "And now you know what we do? I'll teach you to write poems!" I smiled, telling her that maybe I'll never become a poet like her, but I've written a book that I hope can inspire and assist others.

Chapter 1
Fundamentals of Diabetes

Let's embark on this crucial journey together, learning about diabetes. Whether you're here to prevent it or looking for ways to manage it better, our aim is to provide you with straightforward information so you can approach diabetes with confidence. The reason you're here doesn't change the essential truth we need to face: the healthy eating habits recommended for diabetes are really something everyone should aim for. It's all about cutting out the bad stuff that affects us all and choosing balanced, nutritious food options instead. Diabetes can be a stealthy condition, creeping up without noticeable symptoms. But here's the hopeful part: by making small adjustments in your lifestyle, eating well, and staying active, you can prevent or control it effectively. We're going to learn about what diabetes is and its impact on our bodies. And don't worry, we'll keep things simple and understandable, steering clear of complicated medical jargon. So, let's ease into the basics together!

1.1   What is diabetes?

Detes is kind of like a glitch in how our bodies handle energy from food. It boils down to an issue with Diabetes is kind of like a glitch in how our bodies handle energy from food. It boils down to an issue with insulin, this friend protein that's supposed to help sugar get into our cells to fuel them. When there isn't enough insulin, or none at all, our cells don't get the energy they need. This can make us feel really tired and sluggish. Moreover, when sugar piles up in our blood instead of being absorbed by cells, it can start causing trouble for vital organs like the heart, kidneys, and eyes. It's super important to keep diabetes in check to prevent these serious issues down the line and to keep living life to the fullest.

1.2   Types of diabetes:

Imagine your body as a house where energy is the guest that needs to get inside. In Type 1 diabetes, it's as if you've lost the key (insulin) that opens the door to letting energy from food into the cells. Without this key, the house (your body) can't welcome its much-needed guest (energy), leaving you feeling energy-starved. On the other hand, type 2 diabetes is like having a key that's bent or damaged; it exists but struggles to unlock the door, so the energy can't get in as it should, leading to similar feelings of exhaustion. With Type 1 diabetes, we need to find a new key by providing insulin externally, ensuring that energy can enter the cells. For Type 2, it's more about fixing or replacing the faulty key to make sure it can do its job again. This analogy helps peel back the layers of diabetes, highlighting not just the challenges it presents but also underscoring the critical role of managing it well, whether that means replacing the key or repairing it to welcome energy back into our 'house.'

1.3   Impact of Diabetes:

Diabetes isn't just about the physical struggles; it touches every part of life, including how we connect with family and friends. It brings daily hurdles, like keeping blood sugar in check and tweaking what we eat, not to mention the strain it can put on the wallet. My journey with my grandma opened my eyes to how diabetes can stir up family stress and lead to feeling left out or alone. Watching her battle with diabetes showed me how crucial it is for everyone, not just those with the condition, to really understand and be aware of it. Diabetes affects people all over the world, and figuring out how to prevent and manage it better is key to making life better for countless individuals.

Chapter 2
The Diet in Diabetes

The diet for people with diabetes is essential for keeping blood sugar levels in check. I witnessed my grandmother Grace, a woman fond of sweets, learn to make healthier food selections. She started favoring vegetables and cutting back on sweets, reducing her sugar intake. This example illustrates how minor adjustments can significantly impact diabetes management. It wasn't easy for her to give up her beloved treats, but with determination and family support, she discovered new ways to enjoy food. Together, we explored healthy yet tasty recipes, turning mealtime into an opportunity for sharing and discovery. Grandma Grace learned that eating well doesn't mean sacrificing enjoyment; it means relearning to savor it differently. Her journey taught us the importance of adaptability and creative solutions, showing that with effort and a positive attitude, it's possible to manage diabetes without being overwhelmed. Her transformation inspired the whole family to lead healthier lives, emphasizing that taking care of one's health can be a rewarding and unifying journey for everyone.

2.1   Understanding Macronutrients in Diabetes

Julius Caesar once said, "If you can't beat your enemy, make them your friend!" This saying can be cleverly applied to how we view carbohydrates in our diet. Often seen as the enemy, especially in diabetes management, carbs are actually one of the three main building blocks of our food, alongside proteins and fats, providing essential energy for our bodies. They come in different forms: simple carbs, like sugars, that give us quick energy boosts; complex carbs, found in whole grains and veggies, offering sustained energy; and fiber-rich carbs, which are great for our digestion. Finding the right balance of these carbs can be key to keeping our blood sugar levels steady and feeling energized throughout the day. But carbs aren't the only players in the game. Proteins are also crucial allies, helping to keep our blood sugar stable. Incorporating lean protein sources, such as chicken, fish, tofu, or beans, into our meals can make a big difference.

Fats, too, often misunderstood, have a role in managing diabetes. Opting for healthy fats like those found in avocados, nuts, seeds, and olive oil is not only good for the heart, but according to Grandma Grace, it's also the secret to keeping diabetes at bay. She always says that these foods help stabilize blood sugar levels and keep you feeling fuller for longer, thereby aiding in weight management. For those, like her, battling type 2 diabetes and aiming for a healthy weight, it's golden advice. So, by getting to know and manage carbohydrates, along with their buddies' proteins and fats, we're not just making peace with so-called dietary enemies. We're assembling a team of allies to help us live well with diabetes, proving that with the right approach, every nutrient has its place in our strategy for health.

2.2 Using Herbs and Spices for Flavoring

Discovering the power of herbs and spices has been a game-changer in our kitchen adventures. It's amazing how these natural flavor boosters can elevate a meal without the need for extra salt or fat, sparking a whole new level of culinary creativity. From the fresh pop of basil to the earthy depth of rosemary, the zest of cilantro, the warmth of turmeric, and the sweet spice of cinnamon, each one turns the ordinary into something truly extraordinary. Beyond just taste, these kitchen treasures offer a host of health benefits, like antioxidants that support our well-being. As we craft menus with an eye on blood sugar management, we're also exploring exciting spice combinations that promise dishes bursting with flavor, ensuring that eating well means indulging in every delicious bite.

2.2   Supplements

Firmly believing in the power of food as medicine, I want to quote Steve: "let food be your medicine and not medicine be your food." I believe that the most necessary nutrients can be obtained through a balanced and rich diet. Supplements should be a secondary option, and only in specific cases, such as vitamin D, which can be deficient in people living in regions with limited sun exposure because the sun is a natural source of this essential vitamin. For those following a vegan diet, vitamin B12 is crucial, as it is found predominantly in animal-based foods. I recognize the importance of obtaining nutrients from natural sources; vitamin D absorbed directly from the sun is biochemically different from that supplemented. When the skin is exposed to sunlight, it synthesizes sulfated vitamin D3, a form that naturally integrates with body functions, unlike supplements that provide a non-sulfated form, which may be less effective. Vitamin B12, crucial for our well-being, is assimilated by animals mainly through their diet, which includes B12-producing microorganisms present in nature. Herbivores obtain it from plants, while carnivores do so by consuming meat. The human digestive system also hosts bacteria capable of producing B12, but often in a section of the intestine that does not allow effective absorption, making it necessary to intake through fortified foods or supplements. Intensive farming, with its reliance on industrial feeds often lacking in essential nutrients like B12, can limit the availability of this vitamin in animal products. Conversely, animals raised in more natural conditions who can feed on grass, insects, and other B12-rich elements present in the soil tend to have a better nutritional profile. Therefore, it is advisable to opt for products from organic or pasture sources to ensure an optimal B12 intake. For those living in rural areas, choosing eggs and meat from local farms where animals are naturally fed can be a beneficial choice for both health and supporting sustainable farming practices.

2.3   Meal Planning and Order of Consumption

Carefully planning meals is crucial, especially for those managing diabetes. Controlling portion sizes is one of the first steps to avoid excessive fluctuations in blood sugar levels, so initially, you will need to tailor our recipes to your needs, simple with the "Caloric Goals Tables." Food labels are a valuable resource in this regard, as they provide detailed information on calories, carbohydrate, protein, fat, and sugar content per serving. Learning to read and interpret these labels can help make informed decisions on the amount of food to consume. Lastly, establishing regular times for meals and snacks can help keep

blood sugar levels steady throughout the day. Avoiding long periods without food and resisting the temptation to skip meals are important practices in diabetes management. The order of food consumption is also significant. When the meal allows it, start with fiber-rich carbohydrates, then proteins and fats, before moving on to starchy carbohydrates. This slows down the absorption of carbohydrates and stabilizes blood sugar. The frequency of meals is equally important. Divide the calorie intake into small, frequent meals to keep blood sugar stable. Do not skip meals, and include healthy snacks between main meals. I know there are many things to do, but don't worry! Our recipes already include everything.

Chapter 3
What It Means to Live with Diabetes

Living with diabetes is akin to setting off on a journey that requires a solid understanding and a specific set of skills. It's vital to be knowledgeable about the condition and always ready to absorb new information. The key is to remain inquisitive and flexible, recognizing that every day can present new challenges and opportunities for learning. This adventure is not merely about managing a health issue; it represents an ongoing journey of personal growth, increased self-awareness, and constant adjustment. Adopting this perspective can change your experience with diabetes, turning it into an empowering aspect of your life rather than a limitation.

3.1   The Role of Education and Self-Learning

Grasping diabetes isn't just about mastering the fundamental facts. It involves a deeper exploration of how your diet and physical activities impact your blood sugar. But the quest for knowledge doesn't end there. It's equally about becoming attuned to your personal experiences and paying attention to how your body uniquely reacts to various foods and exercises. Each day is an opportunity to discover more about what truly works for you. Navigating through the highs and lows and drawing lessons from successes and setbacks is crucial. It means heeding the subtle and loud signals your body sends, using this insight as a personal compass on your diabetes journey.

3.2   Prevention of Hypoglycemia

Having too low blood sugar, known as hypoglycemia, is a concern for anyone managing diabetes. It's essential to avoid this by carefully planning your meals and snacks. Nonetheless, it's always wise to have a snack on hand. I fondly recall outings with Grandma Grace, where I'd pack a bag with her essentials, and she'd playfully chide me, suggesting I was treating her like a child for being so cautious. What's good to have with you? Options like dried or fresh fruit, whole-grain snacks, or low-glycemic yogurt are great, but remember, moderation is key, unlike my sometimes overly enthusiastic preparations.

3.3   The Importance of Hydration

Water, that magical elixir of life, plays an even more crucial role when it comes to diabetes. Imagine it as a superhero in the world of wellness: not only does it keep our skin glowing and our systems moving, but it also has the special power to help balance blood sugar levels. For those of us living with diabetes, drinking water is not just an act of love for our bodies but an essential daily strategy to keep glucose at bay. So, let's fill up those bottles and make hydration our faithful ally in diabetes management!

3.4   Managing Meals Outdoors

Heading out to eat or planning a family picnic can really influence our blood sugar levels, something I quickly came to realize. The key move I made was getting into the habit of planning ahead. Before stepping out, I make it a point to glance through the restaurant's menu online or decide on picnic foods that fit into a diabetes-friendly diet. And on occasions when planning ahead isn't an option, I've learned to be proactive in asking questions or requesting changes to my order to suit my dietary needs. Maybe it's asking for a meal without added sugar or stressing the need for smaller portions. I've found that restaurant staff are generally more than willing to help out. Learning to speak up about my dietary requirements while dining out has been an invaluable lesson; it's all about advocating for your health with confidence.

Chapter 4
Strategies to Maintain a Healthy Weight

Living with diabetes demands attentive management, and one of the crucial factors for optimal health is maintaining a healthy body weight. Over time, I've gathered valuable strategies to achieve and maintain an ideal weight that helps manage diabetes effectively. In this chapter, we will delve into four essential areas: maintaining nutritional balance, engaging in regular physical activity, tuning into your body's signals, and learning to manage emotional eating. This journey is not just about diet or exercise, but a deep journey of self-listening and understanding, where we learn to differentiate between nourishing our bodies and our souls. By addressing these aspects with care and attention, we'll discover how small changes can lead to significant improvements in diabetes management, enhance our overall well-being, and teach us the importance of balance in every aspect of life. body, and emotional eating management.

4.1 Nutritional balance

Keeping a balanced diet is key to our well-being. It's not necessarily about eliminating certain foods from our lives, but about choosing wisely and managing how much we eat. A healthy diet is rich in diverse, nutrient-packed foods like colorful vegetables, lean sources of protein, and wholesome complex carbs. These are the building blocks our bodies rely on to thrive and maintain good health. For example, rather than banning bread altogether, opting for whole-grain varieties rich in fiber and being mindful of how much we eat can help us manage our blood sugar levels effectively. Embracing variety and moderation allows us to enjoy a wide range of foods while taking care of our health, demonstrating that a balanced approach to eating can support both our physical well-being and our enjoyment of food.

4.2 Regular Physical Activity

Physical activity is a cornerstone for weight control and diabetes management. Regular exercise helps burn excess calories, improve insulin sensitivity, and maintain a healthy body weight. It's not necessary to engage in extreme physical activities; daily walking or yoga sessions can make a significant difference. It yields more results to do 30 minutes a day than 2 hours of intense gym sessions twice a week. Quality and quantity of physical exercise are important, but for a diabetic, the most important element is consistency. Example: Dedicate at least 30 minutes a day to physical activity, such as a walk after dinner or a light dance class. Our diets are organized to meet different caloric needs in a way that leads from a balanced diet to a balanced lifestyle and from sedentariness to constant physical activity.

4.3   Listen to Your Bod

Learning to recognize your body's signals is essential for weight management. Eating slowly, chewing until the food is almost liquid, and listening to satiety signals help us avoid caloric overload. Often, we eat out of habit or stress, so take the time to understand whether we are truly hungry or seeking emotional comfort. Example: Before serving ourselves a second helping, let's pause for a moment and assess whether we are still hungry or satisfiedInizio modulo

4.4   Emotional Eating Management:

How we feel can deeply affect our food choices. It's important to catch ourselves when we're reaching for food because we're stressed or in need of comfort, rather than truly hungry. Instead of letting food be our automatic comfort blanket, we can try other ways to soothe our emotions, like taking up meditation or talking things out with someone who understands. Say stress is getting the better of us; instead of raiding the kitchen, why not pause for a bit of deep breathing, scribble our whirlwind of thoughts into a journal, or maybe start learning meditation? It's about finding those healthier outlets instead of letting stress dictate a beeline to the fridge.

Chapter 5

Safe Freezing and Thawing

Freezing has become a true lifesaver in our kitchen, especially when it comes to cutting down on waste and making meal prep a breeze. It's particularly handy for anyone managing diabetes, offering a way to have healthy meals ready to go. By picking the right containers and mastering a few freezing tricks, you can keep your food tasting great and packed with nutrients. This method isn't just about convenience; it's about making sure you have access to wholesome meals at any time, supporting your health, and simplifying your daily routine.

5.1   Freezing and Thawing Techniques

Quick freezing stands out as a go-to method in our freezing arsenal. It's all about getting your food into the deep chill of the freezer, typically below -18°C (0°F), pretty swiftly. This clever trick stops large ice crystals from forming and messing with the food's texture. When it comes to freezing your favorites safely, reaching for airtight containers or sealing food bags tightly to squeeze out the air is a must, keeping oxidation at bay. These little tips make all the difference in preserving and enjoying your meals just as they were meant to be, even after a thaw.

5.2   Freezing:

* Choose containers that are freezer-friendly to keep your meals tasting just like they were freshly made. Making sure there's no extra air inside helps avoid those pesky ice crystals and freezer burns.
* Splitting your meals into single servings before popping them into the freezer is a real lifesaver. It makes figuring out what's for dinner so much easier and keeps everything organized.
* Letting your hot meals cool down before freezing is a little trick that goes a long way. It helps preserve the deliciousness of your food and ensures your freezer doesn't have to work overtime.

5.3   Thawing:

* Safe thawing occurs slowly in the refrigerator.
* Avoid thawing at room temperature to prevent bacterial growth.
* Use the microwave cautiously for quick thawing. Recommendations:
* Cook foods immediately after thawing.
* Avoid refreezing previously thawed foods unless they have been cooked.
* Ensure that foods are thawed evenly.
* Follow the manufacturer's instructions on frozen foods, especially for ready-to-use options.
* Check the expiration date on frozen foods and consume them before that date.

Chapter 6
Involving Children in Preparation

My grandmother and I have been on this diet journey together for eight years now. Even though I don't have diabetes, I've never felt healthier or more energized. Being so close to someone managing diabetes has shown me how crucial it is for the whole family, kids included, to be part of the health conversation. Getting kids involved in cooking is more than just fun family time—it's a golden opportunity to teach them why eating right matters and to help them form good eating habits from the start.

6.1   10 Tips on How to Make It Fun and Educational:

1. **Assign Specific Roles:** Give children specific roles like "Chef's Assistant" and provide them with accessories such as aprons or chef hats to make the role more authentic.
2. **Creativity in the Kitchen:** Use food for artistic expressions, like creating smiley faces with fruits and vegetables or assembling colorful skewers.
3. **Tell Stories:** Discuss foods in terms of stories, such as explaining how carrots improve vision, making the food more interesting and "magical."
4. **Educational Games:** Incorporate games such as guessing ingredients blindfolded or categorizing food by color or shape.
5. **Sensory Exploration:** Allow children to touch, smell, and taste the ingredients, developing a deep sensory knowledge of food.
6. **Participation in Choosing Ingredients:** Let children participate in choosing ingredients, for example, during grocery shopping.
7. **Gradual Tasks:** Assign tasks appropriate to their age and abilities, like slicing, mixing, adding ingredients, or decorating.
8. **Positive Feedback:** Praise their work and encourage efforts to build their confidence in the kitchen.
9. **Family Traditions:** Establish culinary traditions such as special evenings to involve children.
10. **Showcase Results:** Highlight the importance of their contribution to creating delicious meals.

Chapter 7
Recipe Customization

Our diabetic-friendly recipes are already balanced and designed for a single person. At the end of the book, you will find bonuses and charts to adjust the recipes to your specific situation, age, sports activity, and, last but not least, hunger. But let's get back to the main point: why are our recipes for one person? Well, they simplify everything! If you're single or the only one at home following our recipes, there's no hassle; you won't have to do any calculations. But if you have guests, or even better, if you manage to involve your spouse or your children in healthy eating, you'll just need to double or triple the ingredients based on the number of diners. Remember! Besides health discussions, the more family members you involve, the fewer meals you will have to prepare each day.

To balance the recipes just right, you will find unrounded ingredient quantities, giving you some freedom in preparation while keeping you within the correct macronutrient ratio. For the same reason, if the amounts of a meal seem too much for you, feel free to reduce them slightly; you will still remain within a safe range.

However, finding single-portion ingredients at the supermarket can be challenging. To solve this issue, you will find solutions in the index at the end of the book for using the same ingredients in different recipes or preserving them for future use, thus avoiding waste.

Despite my ambition to include personalized caloric plans in my work, I had to accept that this was not feasible in a book format. However, the main goal has always been to free you from the burden of continuous calculations and measurements, as living with diabetes should never turn into a chain. The recipes I have proposed are designed to let you enjoy cooking peacefully, confident that every ingredient has been carefully chosen and measured for you, regardless of your caloric needs or your size. In my approach to nutrition, I have conceived three distinct paths within my collection of recipes, each designed to adapt to different needs and goals:

7.1 Maintenance:

These recipes are little treasures for those wishing to maintain their ideal weight. They're not just simple dishes but thoughtfully crafted creations, perfectly calibrated to meet your daily nutritional needs without excess, ensuring you receive balanced and comprehensive nourishment. Each recipe is infused with variety, promising to make the journey towards well-being not just healthy but also delightfully tasty, nudging you towards an active and joyful lifestyle.

7.2 BONUS 1 Weight Loss:

If shedding some pounds is your goal, don't miss the special section at the book's end. There, you'll find a QR code to download an extra weight-loss bonus. This bonus is packed with tweaks to the original recipes—think smaller portions and carefully chosen ingredients—all designed to help you achieve the caloric deficit needed for losing weight. Plus, every recipe points you to the exact page where you can dive into the details and how-tos, making sure you don't compromise on flavor or nutrition while on your weight loss journey.

7.3 BONUS 2 Workout:

For individuals with intense physical activity or those who practice sports, the third path proposes an increase in caloric intake. The recipes are enriched to support greater energy needs. Again, at the end of the book, you will find instructions to download the training bonus with a QR code, where the quantities of the ingredients and the reference to the recipe are indicated, along with all the details and preparation instructions. I envision the three paths of my nutritional guide not as separate ways but as stages of a single journey towards well-being. We start with reducing fat mass, then proceed to increase lean mass, accompanied by a gradual increase in calories. This transition is based on carefully chosen and balanced ingredients to nourish us adequately throughout the day, ensuring that each step brings us closer to optimal physical form and a healthier and more harmonious lifestyle.

Are you ready now? Let's move on to practice, and bon Appétit!

Chapter 8
Maintenance Goal Recipes

8.1. Breakfasts

1. Whole Wheat Pancakes with Sugar-Free Maple Syrup

INGREDIENTS: QUANTITY FOR 1 PERSON

- **Whole wheat flour:** 2.41 oz, about ⅔ cup (68.25g)
- **Large egg:** 1.00 oz, about ½ large egg (28.44g)
- **Unsweetened almond milk:** 4.82 oz, about 1 cup (136.51g)
- **Canola oil:** 0.30 oz, about 2 teaspoons (8.53g)
- **Sugar-free maple syrup:** 0.60 oz, about 2 tablespoons (17.06g)
- **Baking powder:** 0.10 oz, about ½ teaspoon (2.84g)

COOKING TIME:

⏱	20 minutes
🍲	10 minutes
🥄	10 minutes
❄	Easy

NUTRITIONAL VALUES (ESTIMATE):

Calories: 400 kcal; **Total Carbohydrates (With Fiber):** 93.64 oz (2654.38g); **Starchy Carbohydrates:** Calculated as part of the total carbohydrates minus fiber; **Fiber:** 13.68 oz (387.58g); **Protein:** 24.5 oz (694.51g); **Fat:** 29.5 oz (836.31g).

MICRONUTRIENTS: IRON, MAGNESIUM, POTASSIUM

INSTRUCTIONS:

1. **Prepare the batter:** In a bowl, mix the whole wheat flour with baking powder. Add the egg, almond milk, and canola oil. Stir until smooth.
2. **Heat the Pan:** Preheat a non-stick pan and lightly grease it with a bit of canola oil.
3. **Cook the Pancakes:** Pour a ladle of batter for each pancake into the hot pan. Cook for about 2-3 minutes per side, or until golden brown and well-cooked inside.
4. **Serve:** Serve the pancakes warm with the sugar-free maple syrup poured over them.

2. Oatmeal, Blueberry, and Cinnamon Muffins

INGREDIENTS: QUANTITY FOR 1 PERSON

- **Oatmeal flour:** 1.78 oz, about ⅔ cup (50.50g)
- **Fresh blueberries:** 0.89 oz, about ⅓ cup (25.25g)
- **Large egg:** 0.89 oz, about ½ large egg (25.25g)
- **Unsweetened almond milk:** 1.07 oz, about 4 tablespoons (30.30g)
- **Coconut oil:** 0.53 oz, about 2 tablespoons (15.15g)
- **Erythritol sweetener:** 0.27 oz, about 1 tablespoon (7.57g)
- **Baking powder:** 0.09 oz, about ½ teaspoon (2.52g)
- **Ground cinnamon:** 0.09 oz, about ½ teaspoon (2.52g)
- **Vanilla extract:** 0.09 oz, about ½ teaspoon (2.52g)

COOKING TIME:

⏱	25 minutes
🍲	15 minutes
🥣	10-12 minutes
❄	Easy

NUTRITIONAL VALUES (ESTIMATE):

Calories: 400 kcal; **Total Carbohydrates (With Fiber):** 1.70 oz (48.15g); **Fiber:** 0.26 oz (7.29g); **Protein:** 0.39 oz (11.09g); **Fats:** 0.77 oz (21.94g); **Sodium:** 0.011 oz (319.89mg).

MICRONUTRIENTS: IRON, MAGNESIUM, POTASSIUM

INSTRUCTIONS:

1. **Prepare the dough:** Take a large bowl, add the oatmeal flour, and mix with the cinnamon and baking powder. Then add the almond milk, egg, vanilla, erythritol, and finally the coconut oil. Now, let's get to it and make everything homogeneous.
2. **Add the Blueberries:** Gently fold the fresh blueberries into the batter to avoid crushing them.
3. **Grease the Muffin Pan:** Take a muffin pan, insert paper liners, and grease them if necessary with a bit of coconut oil.
4. **Bake the Muffins:** Transfer the batter into the ready muffin cups, filling them up to about three-quarters full. Place them in an oven preheated to 180°C (350°F) for about 10-12 minutes. They will be ready when you can insert a toothpick into the center of a muffin and it comes out dry without any batter sticking to it. This is your little sign that they are perfectly baked and ready to be enjoyed.
5. **I'm sorry, you must wait:** Let them cool by leaving them in the pan for just a few minutes; they are good in every way except when piping hot.

3. Spinach and Light Feta Frittata

INGREDIENTS: QUANTITY FOR 1 PERSON:

- **Large eggs:** 3.71 oz, about 2 large eggs (105.10g)
- **Fresh spinach:** 2.22 oz, about 1 cup (63.06g)
- **Light feta:** 1.11 oz, about ⅓ cup (31.53g)
- **Olive oil:** 0.56 oz, about 1 tablespoon (15.76g)

COOKING TIME:

⏱	15 minutes
🍲	5 minutes
🥣	10 minutes
❄	Easy

NUTRITIONAL VALUES (ESTIMATE):

Calories: 400 kcal; **Total Carbohydrates (With Fiber):** 0.16 oz (4.46g); **Fiber:** 0.05 oz (1.32g); **Proteins:** 0.67 oz (18.94g); **Fats:** 1.14 oz (32.24g); **Sodium:** 0.018 oz (506.2mg).

MICRONUTRIENTS: IRON, MAGNESIUM, POTASSIUM

INSTRUCTIONS:

1. **Prep Time:** Whisk the eggs in a bowl. Give the spinach a quick wash and chop it up. Then, crumble that feta cheese.
2. **Pan's Ready:** Heat up some olive oil in a pan over a medium flame.
3. **Frittata Magic:** Throw the spinach into the pan just until it softens. Next, pour the eggs over them and sprinkle the feta on top. Cook it for 5 minutes until the bottom is solid, then flip it over and cook for another 5 minutes until it's all set.
4. **Serve and enjoy:** Cut the frittata into slices and serve it warm.

4. Avocado Toast with Poached Egg and Turmeric

INGREDIENTS: QUANTITY FOR 1 PERSON

- **Whole wheat bread:** 2.12 oz, about 1 and ⅓ cup (60.0g)
- **Avocado:** 3.53 oz, about ½ medium avocado (100g)
- **Egg:** 1.76 oz, about 1 large egg (50g)
- **Turmeric powder:** 0.04 oz, about ¼ teaspoon (1g)
- **Chili pepper to taste:** negligible quantity for caloric purposes

COOKING TIME:

⏱	10 minutes
🍲	5 minutes
🥄	5 minutes
❄	Easy

NUTRITIONAL VALUES (ESTIMATE):

Calories: 400 kcal; **Total Carbohydrates (With Fiber):** 1.39 oz (39.59g); **Fiber:** 0.40 oz (11.41g); **Proteins:** 0.58 oz (16.38g); **Fats:** 0.81 oz (23.00g); **Sodium:** 0.013 oz (369.30mg).

MICRONUTRIENTS: IRON, MAGNESIUM, POTASSIUM

INSTRUCTIONS:

1. **Prepare the Bread and Avocado:** Toast the slice of whole wheat bread until it becomes crispy yet still soft inside. Lightly mash the avocado in a bowl and spread it evenly over the entire surface of the toasted bread.
2. **Poach the egg:** boil the right amount of water to immerse an egg in a small pot, gently crack the egg into it, cook the egg for 3 minutes or longer if you like it firmer, and when it's ready, remove it from the water with a slotted spoon.
3. **Complete the toast:** Place the poached egg on top of the avocado spread on the bread. Sprinkle with chili pepper to taste and a dusting of turmeric powder for a touch of color and flavor.
4. **Serve:** Enjoy your avocado and poached egg toast immediately, benefiting from the rich, spicy flavors as well as the beneficial properties of turmeric.

5. Greek Yogurt with Nuts, Honey, Almonds, and Chia Seeds

INGREDIENTS: QUANTITY FOR 1 PERSON

- **Fat-free Greek yogurt:** 5.70 oz, about 1 and ⅔ cup (161.53g)
- **Chopped nuts:** 0.85 oz, about ⅓ cup (24.23g)
- **Honey:** 0.43 oz, about 1 tablespoon (12.12g) do not overdo it
- **Sliced almonds:** 0.43 oz, about 1 tablespoon (12.12g)
- **Chia seeds:** 0.28 oz, about 2 tablespoons (8.08g)

COOKING TIME:

⏱	5 minutes
🍲	5 minutes
🥄	Not applicable
❄	Easy

NUTRITIONAL VALUES (ESTIMATE):

Calories: 400 kcal; **Total Carbohydrates (With Fiber):** 1.39 oz (39.59g); **Fiber:** 0.21 oz (5.90g); **Proteins:** 0.84 oz (23.76g); **Fats:** 0.88 oz (24.97g); **Sodium:** 0.002 oz (68.61mg).

MICRONUTRIENTS: IRON, MAGNESIUM, POTASSIUM

INSTRUCTIONS:

1. **Prepare the base:** Pour the Greek yogurt into a medium bowl.
2. **Add Nuts and Almonds:** Sprinkle the yogurt with chopped nuts and sliced almonds, distributing them evenly to create a crunchy layer.
3. **Incorporate Chia Seeds:** Add the chia seeds on top of the nuts and almonds layer to enrich the dish with additional nutrients and texture.
4. **Sweeten with Honey:** Gently pour the honey over the dry ingredients, creating a spiral for a sweet and visually appealing touch, but do not overdo it.
5. **Serve:** Lightly stir before serving to combine the flavors, or leave the layers distinct for a visual and textural effect. Enjoy this nutritious and delicious dish as a healthy breakfast or snack.

6. Bell Pepper and Light Cheddar Omelette with Whole Wheat Bread

INGREDIENTS: QUANTITY FOR 1 PERSON

- **Egg whites:** 3.49 oz, about 3 large egg whites (99g)
- **Diced red bell peppers:** 1.76 oz, about ½ cup (50g)
- **Grated light cheddar:** 1.06 oz, about ¼ cup (30g)
- **Olive oil:** 0.53 oz, about 1 tablespoon (15g)
- **Whole wheat bread:** 2.05 oz, about 1 and a half slices (58.12g)

COOKING TIME:

15 minutes

5 minutes

10 minutes

Easy

NUTRITIONAL VALUES (ESTIMATE):

Calories: 402 kcal; **Total Carbohydrates (With Fiber):** 1.12 oz (31.91g); **Fiber:** 0.17 oz (4.92g); **Proteins:** 0.93 oz (26.40g); **Fats:** 0.69 oz (19.72g); **Sodium:** 0.023 oz (645.71mg).

MICRONUTRIENTS: IRON, MAGNESIUM, POTASSIUM

INSTRUCTIONS:

1. **Prepare the ingredients:** In a bowl, lightly beat the egg whites. Dice the red bell peppers and grate the light cheddar.
2. **Heat the Pan:** Heat the oil in a pan over medium heat.
3. **Cook Omelet:** Add the egg whites to the hot pan. Add the diced red bell peppers, and let the omelet start to set. Before it is fully cooked, sprinkle the grated light cheddar over one half of the omelet, then fold it in half to close.
4. **Toast the Bread:** While the omelet is cooking, toast the slices of whole wheat bread in a toaster or on a grill until they are crispy yet still soft inside.
5. **Serve:** Serve the hot omelet accompanied by the slices of toasted whole wheat bread.

7. Quinoa and Cinnamon Porridge with Apples and Bananas

INGREDIENTS: QUANTITY FOR 1 PERSON

- **Quinoa:** 1.76 oz, about ⅔ cup (50g)
- **Unsweetened almond milk:** 8.82 oz, about 1 and ¼ cups (250ml)
- **Cinnamon:** 0.18 oz, about 1 teaspoon (5ml)
- **Erythritol sweetener:** 0.53 oz, about 1 tablespoon (15ml)
- **Apples:** 3.53 oz, about ¾ cup (100g)
- **Bananas:** 3.53 oz, about ¾ cup (100g)

COOKING TIME:

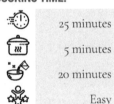

25 minutes

5 minutes

20 minutes

Easy

NUTRITIONAL VALUES (ESTIMATE):

Calories: 386.98 kcal; **Total Carbohydrates (With Fiber):** 1.31 oz (37.0g); **Fiber:** 0.18 oz (5.0g); **Proteins:** 0.05 oz (1.4g); **Fats:** 0.02 oz (0.5g); **Sodium:** 0.00007 oz (2mg).

MICRONUTRIENTS: IRON, MAGNESIUM, POTASSIUM (NATURALLY PRESENT IN QUINOA, APPLES, AND BANANAS)

INSTRUCTIONS:

1. **Prepare the Ingredients:** In a medium bowl, lightly beat the egg whites. Dice the red bell peppers and grate the light cheddar.
2. **Heat the Pan:** Heat the olive oil in a non-stick pan over medium heat. Ensure the oil evenly coats the bottom of the pan.
3. **Cook the Omelette:** Pour the egg whites into the hot pan. Add the diced red bell peppers and let the omelette start to set. Before it is fully cooked, sprinkle the grated light cheddar over one half of the omelette, then fold it in half to close.
4. **Toast the Bread:** While the omelette is cooking, toast the slices of whole wheat bread in a toaster or on a grill until they are crispy yet still soft inside.
5. **Serve:** Serve the hot omelette accompanied by the slices of toasted whole wheat bread

8. Whole waffles with fresh fruit.

INGREDIENTS: QUANTITY FOR 1 PERSON

- **Whole wheat flour:** 2.32 oz, about ⅔ cup (65.82g)
- **Large egg:** 1.16 oz, about 1 large egg (32.91g)
- **Unsweetened almond milk:** 4.64 oz, about 1 and ¾ cups (131.63ml)
- **Canola oil:** 0.35 oz, about 1 tablespoon (9.87ml)
- **Fresh fruit of choice:** 1.16 oz, about ¾ cup (32.91g)
- **Baking powder:** 0.12 oz, about ⅓ teaspoon (3.29g)

COOKING TIME:

⏱	20 minutes
🍲	10 minutes
🥣	10 minutes
❄	Easy

NUTRITIONAL VALUES (ESTIMATE):

Calories: 400 kcal; **Total Carbohydrates (With Fiber):** 1.90 oz (53.71g); **Fiber:** 0.26 oz (7.24g); **Proteins:** 0.48 oz (13.66g); **Fats:** 0.59 oz (16.65g); **Sodium:** 0.016 oz (454.66mg).

MICRONUTRIENTS: IRON, MAGNESIUM, POTASSIUM

INSTRUCTIONS:

1. **Mixing It Up:** Grab a big bowl and whisk together your whole wheat flour and baking powder. Toss in the egg, almond milk, and canola oil, and mix until everything's nice and smooth.
2. **Waffle Iron Time:** Turn on your waffle iron to get it hot and give it a quick brush with some canola oil.
3. **Waffle Making:** Scoop some batter into the waffle iron for each waffle. Shut it and let them cook for 4-5 minutes, or until they're crispy on the outside and fluffy inside.
4. **Ready to Eat:** Dish out those warm waffles with a handful of fresh fruit tossed on top for extra yum.

9. Whole Wheat Pancakes with Sugar-Free Maple Syrup

INGREDIENTS: QUANTITY FOR 1 PERSON

- **Whole wheat flour:** 2.41 oz, about ⅔ cup (68.25g)
- **Large egg:** 1.00 oz, about ½ large egg (28.44g)
- **Unsweetened almond milk:** 4.82 oz, about 1 cup (136.51g)
- **Canola oil:** 0.30 oz, about 2 teaspoons (8.53g)
- **Sugar-free maple syrup:** 0.60 oz, about 2 tablespoons (17.06g)
- **Baking powder:** 0.10 oz, about ½ teaspoon (2.84g)

COOKING TIME:

⏱	20 minutes
🍲	10 minutes
🥣	10 minutes
❄	Easy

NUTRITIONAL VALUES (PER SERVING):

Calories: 400 kcal; **Total Carbohydrates (With Fiber):** 93.64 oz (2654.38g) to be reviewed; **Fiber:** 13.68 oz (387.58g); **Proteins:** 24.5 oz (694.51g); **Fats:** 29.5 oz (836.31g); **Sodium:** 0.015 oz (427 mg).

MICRONUTRIENTS: CONTAINS IRON, MAGNESIUM, AND POTASSIUM, THANKS TO THE NATURAL PRESENCE IN WHOLE WHEAT FLOUR AND OTHER INGREDIENTS.

INSTRUCTIONS:

1. **Batter Time:** In a big bowl, mix up the whole wheat flour and baking powder. Crack in the egg, pour in the almond milk and canola oil, and stir until it's all smooth.
2. **Pan Prep:** Get a non-stick pan warm over medium heat and swipe it with a bit of canola oil.
3. **Pancake Magic:** Ladle the batter into the warm pan, making pancakes. Let them cook for 2-3 minutes on each side until they're golden and cooked through. Keep going until you're out of batter.
4. **Enjoy:** Pile your pancakes on a plate and drizzle them with sugar-free maple syrup.

10. Breakfast Burrito with Turkey and Avocado

INGREDIENTS: QUANTITY FOR 1 PERSON

- **Whole wheat tortilla:** 2.49 oz, about 1 tortilla (70.52g)
- **Ground turkey breast:** 2.07 oz, about ⅔ cup (58.77g)
- **Avocado:** 2.07 oz, about ½ large avocado (58.77g)
- **Egg whites:** 2.74 oz, about 2 large egg whites (77.57g)
- **Hot sauce to taste:** negligible amount for calorie purposes

COOKING TIME:

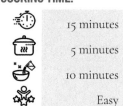

- 15 minutes
- 5 minutes
- 10 minutes
- Easy

NUTRITIONAL VALUES (ESTIMATE):

Calories: 400 kcal; **Total Carbohydrates (With Fiber):** 2.82 oz (40.11g); **Fiber:** 0.34 oz (9.58g); **Protein:** 2.07 oz (29.45g); **Fats:** 0.55 oz (15.71g); **Sodium:** 0.020 oz (573.62mg).

MICRONUTRIENTS: IRON, MAGNESIUM, POTASSIUM

INSTRUCTIONS:

1. **Prepare the Ingredients:** In a skillet, cook the ground turkey breast until fully cooked. In another skillet, cook the egg whites until they are soft and fluffy.
2. **Heat the Tortilla:** Lightly warm the whole wheat tortilla in a pan to make it softer and more flexible.
3. **Assemble the burrito:** On the tortilla, first place the cooked turkey, then the egg whites and sliced avocado. Add hot sauce to taste.
4. **Roll the burrito:** Fold the sides of the tortilla towards the center, and then roll tightly to close the burrito.
5. **Serve:** Enjoy your warm breakfast burrito, accompanied by additional hot sauce if desired.

11. Toast with Ricotta and Grilled Peaches

INGREDIENTS: QUANTITY FOR 1 PERSON:

- **Whole wheat bread:** 2.12 oz, about 2 slices (60g)
- **Light ricotta:** 4.23 oz, about ½ cup (120g)
- **Grilled peaches:** 5.29 oz, about 1 large peach and ½ (150g)

COOKING TIME:

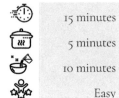

- 15 minutes
- 5 minutes
- 10 minutes
- Easy

NUTRITIONAL VALUES (ESTIMATE):

Calories: 372.3 kcal; **Total Carbohydrates:** 43.2g; **Fiber:** 5.85g; **Protein:** 22.5g; **Fats:** 14.25g; **Sodium:** 394.8mg.

MICRONUTRIENTS: IRON, MAGNESIUM, POTASSIUM, VITAMIN A, B VITAMINS

INSTRUCTIONS:

1. **Grill the Peaches:** Cut a peach in half, remove the pit, and grill the halves on a hot grill until they are soft and have the characteristic grill marks.
2. **Toast the Bread:** Toast the whole wheat bread slices to your desired level of crispiness.
3. **Assemble the Toast:** Evenly spread the light ricotta on the toasted bread slices.
4. **Add the Peaches:** Place the grilled peach halves on top of the ricotta on the bread.
5. **Serve:** Enjoy the warm toast immediately to fully appreciate the combined flavors of creamy ricotta and sweet, slightly charred peaches.

12. Sweet Potato Waffles with Cinnamon and Turmeric

INGREDIENTS: QUANTITY FOR 1 PERSON:

- **Grated sweet potatoes:** 8.06 oz, about 1 and ½ cup (228g)
- **Egg whites:** 5.32 oz, about 4 egg whites (151g)
- **Olive oil:** 0.40 oz, about 2 teaspoons (11g)
- **Cinnamon:** 0.20 oz, about 1 teaspoon (6g)
- **Turmeric:** 0.10 oz, about ½ teaspoon (3g)

COOKING TIME:

15 minutes

5 minutes

10 minutes

Easy

NUTRITIONAL VALUES (ESTIMATE):

Calories: 400 kcal; **Total Carbohydrates:** 57.06g; **Fiber:** 8.1g; **Protein:** 20.32g; **Fats:** 9.73g; **Sodium:** 347mg.

MICRONUTRIENTS: IRON, MAGNESIUM, MANGANESE, POTASSIUM, VITAMIN A

INSTRUCTIONS:

1. **Whipping Up the Mix:** Grab a big bowl and toss in your grated sweet potatoes, egg whites, a dash of cinnamon, and a pinch of turmeric. Give it a good stir.
2. **Pan Time:** Get your pan nice and hot over a medium flame with a splash of olive oil.
3. **Waffle Creation:** Spoon some of that mixture into the pan, patting it down into a waffle shape. Let it cook until each side is golden and crisp, about 5 minutes.
4. **Ready to Serve:** Dish out those hot waffles with a little extra cinnamon on top for kicks.

13. Whole Wheat Crepes with Ricotta and Raspberries

INGREDIENTS: QUANTITY FOR 1 PERSON:

- **Whole wheat flour:** 2.23 oz, about ⅔ cup (63.11g)
- **Eggs:** 2.23 oz, about 2 large eggs (63.11g)
- **Unsweetened almond milk:** 4.45 oz, about 1 and ¾ cup (126.22ml)
- **Light ricotta:** 1.34 oz, about ⅓ cup (37.87g)
- **Fresh raspberries:** 1.11 oz, about ¾ cup (31.56g)

COOKING TIME:

20 minutes

10 minutes

10 minutes

Easy

NUTRITIONAL VALUES (ESTIMATE):

Calories: 379 kcal; **Total Carbohydrates (With Fiber):** Appropriately increased to maintain the proportions CF 50%, CA 25%, F, and G 25%; **Fiber:** Increased thanks to the use of whole wheat flour and raspberries; **Protein:** Balanced between eggs and light ricotta; **Fats:** Moderate, mainly from eggs and light ricotta; **Sodium:** minimized content, varies based on specific ingredients.

MICRONUTRIENTS: IRON, MAGNESIUM, POTASSIUM, VITAMIN A

INSTRUCTIONS:

1. **Prepare the batter:** In a big mixing bowl, mix the whole wheat flour, eggs, and almond milk until smooth.
2. **Heat the Pan:** Heat a non-stick pan lightly greased with olive oil over medium heat.
3. **Cook the crepes:** When the pan is hot, pour a portion of the batter, then move it around to spread it evenly, making sure there are no holes. Cook one side, then the other, until golden. Repeat until the batter is finished.
4. **Stuff the Crepes:** Spread each crepe with light ricotta and add fresh raspberries on top.
5. **Serve hot:** Fold the crepes in half or roll them up, and serve immediately.

14. Turkey Sausage and Baked Eggs with Smoked Paprika

INGREDIENTS: QUANTITY FOR 1 PERSON:

- **Eggs:** 3.48 oz, about 2 large eggs (98.6g)
- **Turkey sausage, cooked and crumbled:** 1.74 oz, about ½ cup (49.3g)
- **Olive oil:** 0.52 oz, about 1 and ½ tablespoon (14.8g)
- **Smoked paprika:** Not quantified in ounces for nutritional estimate, used for flavor

COOKING TIME:

26 minutes

12 minutes

14 minutes

Easy

NUTRITIONAL VALUES (ESTIMATE):

Calories: 399.5 kcal; **Total Carbohydrates:** 0.056 oz (1.58g); **Protein:** 0.75 oz (21.2g); **Fats:** 1.22 oz (34.52g); **Sodium:** 0.018 oz (517mg).

MICRONUTRIENTS: IRON, MAGNESIUM, POTASSIUM, VITAMIN A

INSTRUCTIONS:

1. **Get Set:** Turn the oven on to warm up to 180°C (350°F). Give your turkey sausage a nice sprinkle of smoked paprika to jazz it up.
2. **Prep the Pan:** Lightly coat a baking dish with olive oil, then lay the seasoned sausage evenly on the bottom.
3. **Egg Time:** Gently break the eggs over the sausage layer, aiming to keep those yolks whole.
4. **Into the Oven:** Slide it into the oven and bake until the eggs are just how you like them, which should take about 15 minutes.
5. **Ready to Enjoy:** Serve it straight from the oven, with a little more smoked paprika sprinkled on top for that final flair.

15. Berry and Chia Seed Smoothie Bowl

INGREDIENTS: QUANTITY FOR 1 PERSON:

- **Unsweetened Coconut milk:** 4.47 oz, about 1 and ½ cup (126.62g)
- **Mixed berries (strawberries, blueberries, raspberries):** 1.12 oz, about ⅓ cup (31.66g)
- **Chia seeds:** 0.67 oz, about 2 tablespoons and 1 teaspoon (18.99g)
- **Erythritol sweetener:** 0.33 oz, about 1 tablespoon (9.50g)

COOKING TIME:

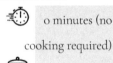

0 minutes (no cooking required)

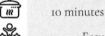

10 minutes

Easy

NUTRITIONAL VALUES (ESTIMATE):

Calories: 387 kcal; **Total Carbohydrates (With Fiber):** About 1.59 oz (45g); **Fiber:** About 0.85 oz (24g); **Protein:** About 0.74 oz (21g); **Fats:** About 1.22 oz (34.5g); **Sodium:** Minimal, varies based on specific ingredients.

MICRONUTRIENTS: IRON, MAGNESIUM, MANGANESE, POTASSIUM, VITAMIN A

INSTRUCTIONS:

1. **Berry Prep:** Toss those fresh berries into a bowl. Feel free to chop them up if you like them bite-sized.
2. **Chia and Coconut Combo:** Grab another bowl and mix your chia seeds with coconut milk. Let it sit for a bit, around 5 minutes, so the chia seeds get all plump.
3. **Sweeten the Mix:** Stir some erythritol into your chia-coconut mix to sweeten it up.
4. **Smoothie Bowl Assembly:** Pour your chia mixture into a bowl and scatter your berries right on top.
5. **Chill and Enjoy:** Dive in right away to keep things cool and fresh.

8.2. Lunch

16. Mediterranean Chicken Salad with Whole Wheat Bread

INGREDIENTS: QUANTITY FOR 1 PERSON:

- **Grilled Chicken:** 3.53 oz (100g)
- **Romaine Lettuce:** 5.29 oz, about 3 cups chopped (150g)
- **Tomatoes:** 3.53 oz, about 1 cup (100g)
- **Cucumbers:** 3.53 oz, about 1 cup (100g)
- **Olives:** 1.06 oz, about ¼ cup (30g)
- **Extra Virgin Olive Oil:** 1 tablespoon (15ml)
- **Oregano:** ½ teaspoon (1g)
- **Garlic Powder:** ½ teaspoon (1g)
- **Ground Fennel Seeds:** ½ teaspoon (1g)
- **Freshly Chopped Rosemary:** about ½ teaspoon (1g)
- **Freshly Chopped Basil:** about 1 teaspoon (2g)
- **Whole Wheat Bread:** 2 thin slices 1.8oz (54g)

COOKING TIME:

⏱	20 minutes
🍲	10 minutes
🥄	10 minutes
❀	Easy

NUTRITIONAL VALUES (ESTIMATE):

Kcal: ~500 kcal; **CF (Carbs with Fiber):** 1.23 oz (35g); **CA (Starchy Carbs):** 0.99 oz (28g); **F (Fats):** 0.74 oz (21g); **P (Proteins):** 0.81 oz (23g); **S (Sodium):** Varies depending on added salt.

MICRONUTRIENTS: VITAMIN A, VITAMIN C, POTASSIUM, FIBER

INSTRUCTIONS:

1. **Ready the Chicken:** Give your chicken breasts a good sprinkle with garlic powder, fennel seeds, and some freshly chopped rosemary before they hit the grill.
2. **Grilling Time:** Fire up the grill and cook those chicken breasts until they're perfectly done.
3. **Veggie Prep:** Give the romaine lettuce a good wash and slice it into ribbons.
4. **Dice Up:** Chop the tomatoes and cucumbers into bite-sized pieces.
5. **Olive Work:** Pit those olives and slice them up.
6. **Dressing Mix:** Whisk together extra virgin olive oil, oregano, garlic powder, fennel seeds, rosemary, and basil in a bowl to craft your dressing.
7. **Salad Assembly:** Toss the grilled chicken, lettuce, tomatoes, cucumbers, and olives in a large salad bowl.
8. **Dressing Time:** Pour your homemade dressing over the salad and give it a good mix.
9. **Serve It Up:** Plate your salad with a couple of slices of whole wheat bread on the side.

17. Baked Salmon with Vegetables

INGREDIENTS: QUANTITY FOR 1 PERSON:

- **Salmon:** 4.94 oz (140g)
- **Broccoli:** 5.29 oz, about 2 cups cut (150g)
- **Carrots:** 3.53 oz, about ¾ cup cut (100g)
- **Extra Virgin Olive Oil:** about 1½ tablespoons (20g)
- **Fresh Grated Ginger:** about 1 teaspoon (5g)
- **Fresh Chopped Garlic:** about 1 teaspoon (5g)
- **Sweet Paprika:** about ½ teaspoon (2g)
- **Fresh Thyme:** about 1 teaspoon chopped (2g)
- **Ground Black Pepper:** about ½ teaspoon (1g)
- **Grated Lemon Zest:** to taste

COOKING TIME:

30 minutes	
15 minutes	
15 minutes	
Medium	

NUTRITIONAL VALUES (ESTIMATE):

Total Calories: About 472 Kcal; **Carbs with Fiber (CF):** About 0.67 oz (19g); **Starchy Carbs (CA):** Practically absent; **Fats (F):** About 0.95 oz (27g); **Proteins (P):** About 0.95 oz (27g); **Sodium (S):** Varies depending on added salt.

MICRONUTRIENTS: VITAMIN A, VITAMIN C, POTASSIUM, FIBER

INSTRUCTIONS:

1. **Spice Up the Salmon:** Rub the salmon with a mix of grated ginger, chopped garlic, paprika, thyme, black pepper, and a zest of lemon.
2. **Let It Sit:** Marinate it for a cozy 30 minutes.
3. **Oven Ready:** Heat your oven up to 356°F (180°C).
4. **Salmon Time:** Pop the salmon in a baking dish and let the oven work its magic for about 15 minutes.
5. **Veggie Prep:** Chop up the broccoli into florets and slice the carrots into sticks.
6. **Cook the Greens:** Choose to either steam or bake those veggies until they're just right—tender and tasty.
7. **Plate It:** Lay out the salmon with the veggies on the side.
8. **Final Touch:** A gentle drizzle of extra virgin olive oil brings it all together.

18. Lentil Soup

INGREDIENTS: QUANTITY FOR 1 PERSON:

- **Lentils:** 4.23 oz (about ¾ cup) (120g)
- **Broccoli:** 5.29 oz (about 2 cups cut) (150g)
- **Carrots:** 3.53 oz (about ¾ cup cut) (100g)
- **Extra Virgin Olive Oil:** about 1¾ tablespoons (25g)
- **Fresh Grated Ginger:** about 1 teaspoon (5g)
- **Fresh Chopped Garlic:** about 1 teaspoon (5g)
- **Sweet Paprika:** about ½ teaspoon (2g)
- **Fresh Thyme:** about 1 teaspoon chopped (2g)
- **Grated Lemon Zest:** to taste
- **Vegetable Broth:** 20.29 oz (about 2½ cups) (600ml)

COOKING TIME:

30-35 minutes

15 minutes

15-20 minutes

Easy

NUTRITIONAL VALUES (ESTIMATE):

Kcal: About 500 kcal; **CF (Carbs with Fiber):** 2.65 oz (75g); **CA (Starchy Carbs):** 0.88 oz (25g); **F (Fats):** 1.06 oz (30g); **P (Proteins):** 1.06 oz (30g); **S (Sodium):** Varies depending on added salt, approximate estimate between 0.053-0.141 oz (1.500-4.000 mg).

MICRONUTRIENTS: VITAMIN A, VITAMIN C, POTASSIUM, FIBER

INSTRUCTIONS:

1. **Soften the Lentils:** Rinse the lentils and, if necessary, soak them for a short period.
2. **Chop and Slice:** Finely chop the celery and carrots.
3. **In a Pot:** Briefly sauté chopped ginger and garlic in extra virgin olive oil.
4. **Mix:** Add the lentils, celery, and carrots to the pot.
5. **Boil:** Pour in the vegetable broth and bring to a boil.
6. **Simmer:** Lower the heat and let simmer to soften the lentils (about 15-20 minutes).
7. **To Season:** Add paprika, thyme, and lemon zest.
8. **Serve:** hot, adjust salt to taste but go easy on it.

19. Tofu and Vegetables Stir-Fry with Beneficial Spices

INGREDIENTS: QUANTITY FOR 1 PERSON

- **Tofu:** 5.29 oz (about 1 1/2 cup chopped) (150g)
- **Bell Peppers:** 3.53 oz (about 1 cup) (100g)
- **Zucchini:** 3.53 oz (about 1 cup) (100g)
- **Low-Sodium Soy Sauce:** 1 tablespoon (15ml)
- **Sesame Oil:** 0.35 oz (about 2 teaspoons) (10g)
- **Garlic Powder:** 1/2 teaspoon (1g)
- **Turmeric:** 1 teaspoon (2g)
- **Fresh Grated Ginger:** 1 teaspoon (2g)

COOKING TIME:

15 minutes

5 minutes

10 minutes

Easy

NUTRITIONAL VALUES (ESTIMATE):

Kcal: About 486 kcal; **CF (Carbs with Fiber):** 0.54 oz (15g); **CA (Starchy Carbs):** 0.03 oz (1g); **F (Fats):** 1.26 oz (35g); **P (Proteins):** 1.08 oz (30g); **S (Sodium):** Varies depending on the soy sauce used.

MICRONUTRIENTS: VITAMIN C, MAGNESIUM, IRON, FIBER

INSTRUCTIONS:

1. **Tofu Time:** Chop the tofu into neat little cubes.
2. **Veggie Sizzle:** Heat up some sesame oil in a skillet, toss in the bell peppers and zucchini slices, and stir-fry them until they're just the right mix of tender and crunchy.
3. **Tofu Toss-In:** Bring the tofu into the mix with the veggies and give it a good stir.
4. **Spice It Up:** Sprinkle in some garlic powder, turmeric, and a bit of freshly grated ginger, stirring to get those flavors mingling.
5. **Soy Splash:** Drizzle the soy sauce over everything, give it another stir, and let it cook for a minute or two more.
6. **Dish Out:** Serve it steaming hot, maybe with a side of brown rice or quinoa to round out the meal

20. Quinoa and Black Bean Salad with Corn and Avocado

INGREDIENTS: QUANTITY FOR 1 PERSON

- **Cooked Quinoa:** 4.88 oz (about 3/4 cup, 138.27g)
- **Black Beans:** 6.70 oz (about 1 cup, 190.01g)
- **Cherry Tomatoes:** 14.11 oz (about 2 cups, 400g)
- **Corn:** 5.47 oz (about 3/4 cup, 155.01g)
- **Avocado:** 2.12 oz (about 1/3 of a medium avocado, 60g)
- **Cilantro:** to taste (negligible quantity)

COOKING TIME:

20 minutes

10 minutes

10 minutes

Easy

NUTRITIONAL VALUES (ESTIMATE):

Kcal: About 500 kcal; **CF (Carbs with Fiber):** 2.78 oz (79g); **CA (Starchy Carbs):** 1.51 oz (43g); **F (Fats):** 1.52 oz (43g); **P (Proteins):** 2.26 oz (64g); **S (Sodium):** Varies depending on added salt.

MICRONUTRIENTS: VITAMIN C, POTASSIUM, FIBER

INSTRUCTIONS:

1. **Quinoa Ready:** Cook the quinoa as the box says, then let it cool off.
2. **Beans Next:** Give the black beans a good rinse and drain them.
3. **Tomato Time:** Wash and slice the cherry tomatoes in half.
4. **Corn Prep:** Drain the corn and warm it up a bit if you like.
5. **Avocado Chop:** Cut up the avocado into cubes.
6. **Toss Together:** Throw the quinoa, black beans, tomatoes, corn, and avocado into a big salad bowl.
7. **Cilantro Touch:** Sprinkle in some fresh cilantro as much as you fancy.
8. **Mix It Up:** Stir everything together nicely.
9. **Serve and Enjoy:** Dish out the salad nice and fresh.

21. Chicken and Couscous Salad with Grilled Vegetables

INGREDIENTS: QUANTITY FOR 1 PERSON

- **Grilled Chicken Breast:** 5.49 oz (155.52g)
- **Cooked couscous:** 5.49 oz (155.52g)
- **Zucchini:** 5.49 oz, about 1 1/2 cups (155.52g)
- **Bell Peppers:** 5.49 oz, about 1 1/2 cups (155.52g)
- **Cumin:** 0.11 oz, about 1 teaspoon (3.11g)

COOKING TIME:

	30 minutes
	15 minutes
	15 minutes
	Medium

NUTRITIONAL VALUES (ESTIMATE):

Kcal: ~500 kcal; **CF (Carbs with Fiber):** 55g (1.94 oz); **CA (Starchy Carbs):** 55g (1.94 oz); **F (Fats):** 11g (0.39 oz); **P (Proteins):** 36g (1.27 oz); **S (Sodium):** Varies depending on added salt.

MICRONUTRIENTS: VITAMIN C, VITAMIN K, POTASSIUM, FIBER

INSTRUCTIONS:

1. **Season That Chicken:** Give your chicken a cozy rub of cumin and salt.
2. **Grill Time:** Fire up the grill and cook that chicken through.
3. **Couscous Magic:** Get the couscous ready, just like the package says.
4. **Char the Veggies:** Throw zucchini and bell peppers on the grill until they're nice and soft.
5. **Salad Toss:** Mix the grilled chicken, couscous, and veggies in a bowl.
6. **Add Some Shine:** Splash on some olive oil and give it a good mix.
7. **Plate and Dig In:** Lay it out on a plate and enjoy it warm or cool.

22. Mushroom Risotto

INGREDIENTS: QUANTITY FOR 1 PERSON

- **Arborio Rice:** 3.53 oz (100g) (uncooked)
- **Mushrooms:** 7.05 oz (200g) (sliced)
- **Chicken Broth:** 22.93 oz (650ml)
- **Onion:** 1.76 oz (50g) (chopped)
- **Parmesan Cheese:** 1.41 oz (40g) (grated)
- **Sage:** 0.18 oz (5g) (chopped)
- **Parsley:** 0.18 oz (5g) (chopped)
- **Turmeric:** 0.14 oz (4g)

COOKING TIME:

	54 minutes
	18 minutes
	36 minutes

NUTRITIONAL VALUES (ESTIMATE):

Kcal: ~495 kcal; **CF (Carbs with Fiber):** 1.23 oz (35g); **CA (Starchy Carbs):** 0.99 oz (28g); **F (Fats):** 0.74 oz (21g); **P (Proteins):** 0.81 oz (23g); **S (Sodium):** Varies depending on added salt.

MICRONUTRIENTS: VITAMIN A, VITAMIN C, POTASSIUM, FIBER

INSTRUCTIONS:

1. Start with the rice. Give your Arborio rice a quick rinse under the tap.
2. **Broth Time:** Get that chicken broth boiling, then simmer it on the back burner.
3. **Onion Action:** Sizzle the onion in a pan until it's picking up some color, using a splash of broth to keep things moist.
4. **Mushroom Golden Time:** Fry those mushrooms until they're just right.
5. **Rice Gets a Tan:** Toss in the rice, letting it catch a little toastiness.
6. **Ladle & Stir:** Keep adding that hot broth to the rice bit by bit, stirring with love.
7. **Herbs Meet Cheese:** Once the rice feels just right, stir in your herbs and a good heap of Parmesan.
8. **Dish it Out:** Serve that creamy mushroom risotto steaming hot.

23. Fish Tacos with Avocado and Red Cabbage

INGREDIENTS: QUANTITY FOR 1 PERSON

- **White Fish Fillets:** 6.95 oz (197g)
- **Corn Tortillas:** 2 small (about 1.76 oz per tortilla)
- **Purple Cabbage** 5.78 oz (164g)
- **Avocado:** 1.73 oz (49g)
- **Lime:** for dressing (negligible quantity)
- **Cumin:** 0.11 oz (3g)

COOKING TIME:

20 minutes

10 minutes

10 minutes

Medium

NUTRITIONAL VALUES (ESTIMATE):

Kcal: ~500 kcal; **CF (Carbs with Fiber):** 2.39 oz (68g); **CA (Starchy Carbs):** 1.2 oz (34g); **F (Fats):** 1.47 oz (42g); **P (Proteins):** 1.76 oz (50g); **S (Sodium):** Varies depending on added salt.

MICRONUTRIENTS: VITAMIN C, VITAMIN E, POTASSIUM, OMEGA-3

INSTRUCTIONS:

1. **Fish Flavor-Up:** Sprinkle a little cumin and a zigzag of olive oil on the fish before it hits the grill.
2. **Grill Duty:** Cook the fish on a hot grill until it's just perfect.
3. **Cabbage Crunch:** Shred that red cabbage fine; toss it with a pinch of salt and a squeeze of lime.
4. **Avocado Slices:** Cut the avocado into slim pieces.
5. **Tortilla Time:** Get those tortillas warmed up, either in a pan or over the grill.
6. **Taco Build:** Lay the grilled fish on the tortillas, top with the zesty cabbage and avocado.
7. **Ready to Serve:** Hand them out with lime wedges for that extra zing.

24. Smoked Salmon Salad

INGREDIENTS: QUANTITY FOR 1 PERSON

- **Smoked Salmon:** 5.64 oz (160g)
- **Green Salad:** 10.58 oz, about 6 cups (300g)
- **Avocado:** 2.12 oz (60g)
- **Cucumbers:** 3.53 oz, about 1 cup (100g)
- **Balsamic Vinegar:** 0.68 oz, about 2 tablespoons (20ml)
- **Turmeric:** 0.11 oz (about 3g)

COOKING TIME:

15 minutes

10 minutes

5 minutes

Easy

NUTRITIONAL VALUES (ESTIMATE):

Kcal: ~500 kcal; **CF (Carbohydrates with Fiber):** 1.52 oz (43g); **CA (Starchy Carbohydrates):** 0.46 oz (13g); **F (Fats):** 1.48 oz (42g); **P (Proteins):** 1.62 oz (46g); **S (Sodium):** Varies depending on added salt.

MICRONUTRIENTS: OMEGA-3, VITAMIN D, VITAMIN E, POTASSIUM, FIBER

INSTRUCTIONS:

1. **Get the Greens Ready:** Give your lettuce a quick rinse and towel-off, then tear it into bite-sized pieces. Thinly slice up the cucumber and chop the avocado into chunks.
2. **Toss the Green Mix:** Throw your lettuce, cucumber, and avocado into a salad bowl. Dash in a bit of turmeric for some color and a healthy kick.
3. **Salmon Time:** Layer the smoked salmon over your salad pile.
4. **Finishing Touch:** Drizzle with balsamic and serve it up fresh and crunchy for a no-fuss, nourishing bite.

25. Vegetable Frittata

INGREDIENTS: QUANTITY FOR 1 PERSON

- **Egg:** 3.53 oz (100g, about 2 large)
- **Spinach:** 3.53 oz, about 2 cups (100g)
- **Tomatoes:** 1.76 oz, about 1/2 cup (50g)
- **Onion:** 1.76 oz, about 1/2 cup (50g)
- **Bell Peppers:** 1.76 oz, about 1/2 pepper (50g)
- **Turmeric:** 0.11 oz (3g, about 1 teaspoon)
- **Extra Virgin Olive Oil:** 1 tablespoon (15ml)
- **Whole Wheat Bread:** 1.76 oz, about 1 slice (50g)

COOKING TIME:

20 minutes

10 minutes

10 minutes

Easy

NUTRITIONAL VALUES (ESTIMATE):

Kcal: ~500 kcal; **CF (Carbohydrates with Fiber):** 2.65 oz (75g); **CA (Starchy Carbohydrates):** 1.06 oz (30g); **F (Fats):** 1.06 oz (30g); **P (Proteins):** 1.41 oz (40g); **S (Sodium):** Varies depending on added salt.

MICRONUTRIENTS: VITAMIN A, VITAMIN C, POTASSIUM, FIBER

INSTRUCTIONS:

1. **Eggs with a Twist:** Whisk those eggs with a sprinkle of turmeric for a sunny color.
2. **Onion Action:** Get the oil shimmering in a pan and toss in the onion until it's just getting sweet and golden.
3. **Veggie Sizzle:** Throw in the spinach, tomatoes, and bell peppers, chopped up, and let them mingle for a bit.
4. **Egg Pour:** Slide the eggs into the pan and let them cuddle up with the veggies over a gentle heat until the frittata's just set.
5. **Bread's Up:** Pop some whole wheat bread in the toaster for a nice crunch.
6. **Plate and Enjoy:** Serve that frittata nice and warm, with toast on the side, for a cozy meal.

26. Farro Salad with Grilled Vegetables

INGREDIENTS: QUANTITY FOR 1 PERSON

- **Cooked Farro:** 5.29 oz, about 1 1/4 cups (150g)
- **Eggplants:** 2.65 oz, about 3/4 cup (75g)
- **Zucchini:** 2.65 oz, about 3/4 cup (75g)
- **Red Peppers:** 2.65 oz, about 3/4 cup (75g)
- **Extra Virgin Olive Oil:** about 1 tablespoon (15g)
- **Turmeric:** 0.11 oz (about 3g)

COOKING TIME:

25 minutes

10 minutes

15 minutes

Easy

NUTRITIONAL VALUES (ESTIMATE):

Kcal: ~347.97 kcal; **CF (Carbohydrates with Fiber):** 1.52 oz (43.2g); **CA (Starchy Carbohydrates):** 0 oz (0g); **F (Fats):** 0.59 oz (16.8g); **P (Proteins):** 0.25 oz (6.99g); **S (Sodium):** 0.3 oz (8.64mg).

MICRONUTRIENTS: VITAMIN A, VITAMIN C, POTASSIUM, FIBER

INSTRUCTIONS:

1. **Veggie Prep:** Toss eggplants, zucchini, and bell peppers with a hint of turmeric and a splash of olive oil before hitting the grill.
2. **Get Grilling:** Cook them until they're tender and sporting those lovely charred edges.
3. **Farro Time:** Whip up the farro just like the bag says.
4. **Toss Together:** In a big bowl, mix the farro with the grilled veggies, drizzle with some more olive oil, and season with a touch of salt.
5. **Mix It Up:** Stir everything well to get those flavors cozying up.
6. **Ready to Serve:** Dish out the salad warm or let it cool to room temperature, topped off with fresh basil or your favorite herbs.

27. Curry Chicken with Brown Rice and Vegetables

INGREDIENTS: QUANTITY FOR 1 PERSON

- **Chicken Breast:** 3.53 oz (100g)
- **Cooked Brown Rice:** 3.53 oz (100g)
- **Coconut Milk:** 1.76 oz, about 1/3 cup (50ml)
- **Curry Powder:** 0.18 oz (5g, about 1 teaspoon)
- **Mixed Vegetables (broccoli, carrots):** 3.53 oz (100g)
- **Ginger:** 0.04 oz, about 1 teaspoon (1g)
- **Extra Virgin Olive Oil:** 1 tablespoon (15ml)

COOKING TIME:

	30 minutes
	15 minutes
	15 minutes
	Medium

NUTRITIONAL VALUES (ESTIMATE):

Kcal: ~481.25 kcal; **CF (Carbohydrates with Fiber):** 0.39 oz (11.01g); **CA (Starchy Carbohydrates):** 1.23 oz (34.80g); **F (Fats):** 0.62 oz (17.68g); **P (Proteins):** 1.36 oz (38.43g); **S (Sodium):** 5.46 oz (154.8mg).

MICRONUTRIENTS: VITAMIN C, POTASSIUM, FIBER

INSTRUCTIONS:

1. **Spice Up the Chicken:** Coat the chicken breast with curry powder and a hint of ginger.
2. **Sizzle the Chicken:** Warm up some olive oil in a skillet and brown the chicken nicely.
3. **Creamy Coconut:** Pour in coconut milk over the chicken, simmering to soak up the flavors.
4. **Rice on the Side:** Cook the brown rice following the instructions on its package.
5. **Veggie Time:** Get those mixed veggies (think broccoli, carrots) grilled or stewed until they're perfectly tender-crisp.
6. **Plating:** Lay the curry chicken over a fluffy bed of brown rice, with the grilled veggies keeping it company.
7. **Final Touch:** Sprinkle a bit more curry or ginger on top, just to kick it up a notch.

28. Whole Wheat Spaghetti with Tomato and Basil

INGREDIENTS: QUANTITY FOR 1 PERSON

- **Whole Wheat Spaghetti:** 3.53 oz (100g)
- **Tomato Sauce:** 5.29 oz, about 1 cup (150g)
- **Basil:** to taste
- **Garlic:** 1 clove
- **Extra Virgin Olive Oil:** 2 teaspoons (10g)

COOKING TIME:

	30 minutes
	10 minutes
	20 minutes
	Easy

NUTRITIONAL VALUES (ESTIMATE):

Kcal: ~500 kcal; **CF (Carbohydrates with Fiber):** 3.12 oz (88.57g); **CA (Starchy Carbohydrates):** 2.76 oz (78.28g); **F (Fats):** 0.74 oz (21g); **P (Proteins):** 0.81 oz (23g); **S (Sodium):** Varies depending on added salt.

MICRONUTRIENTS: VITAMIN A, VITAMIN C, POTASSIUM, FIBER

INSTRUCTIONS:

1. **Boiling Point:** Get a hefty pot of water up to a rolling boil.
2. **Just a Pinch:** Season the water with a modest sprinkle of salt.
3. **Spaghetti Swim:** Ease the spaghetti into the water, letting it soften and sink.
4. **Garlic's Glow:** Sizzle the chopped garlic in a splash of olive oil until it's fragrant, then pour in the tomato sauce to simmer.
5. **Perfect Timing:** Pull the spaghetti off the heat just a bit early, aiming for that perfect al dente texture.
6. **Saucy Mix:** Drain the spaghetti and lovingly toss it with the simmered sauce.
7. **Meld the Flavors:** Give it a minute to meld together, keeping the sauce from drying out.
8. **Basil Finish:** Serve it up with a garnish of fresh basil on top.

29. Turkey Chili

INGREDIENTS: QUANTITY FOR 1 PERSON

- **Ground Turkey:** 4.67 oz (132.28g)
- **Red Beans:** 3.74 oz (105.82g)
- **Canned Tomatoes:** 4.67 oz (132.28g)
- **Onion:** 2.34 oz (66.14g)
- **Chili Powder:** 0.23 oz (6.57g)
- **Whole Wheat Bread:** 0.74 oz (20.83g)

COOKING TIME:

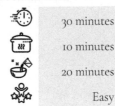

30 minutes
10 minutes
20 minutes
Easy

NUTRITIONAL VALUES (PER SERVING):

Kcal: ~500 kcal; **CF (Carbohydrates with Fiber):** 1.23 oz (35g); **CA (Starchy Carbohydrates):** 0.99 oz (28g); **F (Fats):** 0.74 oz (21g); **P (Proteins):** 0.81 oz (23g); **S (Sodium):** Varies depending on added salt.

MICRONUTRIENTS: VITAMIN A, VITAMIN C, POTASSIUM, FIBER

INSTRUCTIONS:

1. **Onion Start:** Sauté the onion in a pot until it's see-through.
2. **Turkey Time:** Mix in the ground turkey, cooking it until it's thoroughly browned.
3. **Tomato & Bean Mix:** Toss in the canned tomatoes and red beans.
4. **Spice It Up:** Dust it with chili powder for that kick.
5. **Simmer Down:** Let it bubble gently on a medium flame for 20 minutes.
6. **Hot Serving:** Dish out the chili, steaming hot, with slices of whole wheat bread on the side.

30. Quinoa and Chickpea Salad

INGREDIENTS: QUANTITY FOR 1 PERSON

- **Cooked Quinoa:** 7.05 oz (200g)
- **Cooked Chickpeas:** 5.64 oz (160g)
- **Cherry tomatoes:** 3.53 oz (100g)
- **Cucumbers:** 3.53 oz (100g)
- **Lemon:** for dressing
- **Ground Cinnamon:** 1/2 teaspoon (1g)

COOKING TIME:

10 minutes
0 minutes
10 minutes
Easy

NUTRITIONAL VALUES (ESTIMATE):

Kcal: ~510 kcal; **CF (Carbohydrates with Fiber):** 24g; **CA (Starchy Carbohydrates):** 24g; **Fats:** 8g; **Proteins:** 14g; **Sodium:** Varies depending on added salt.

MICRONUTRIENTS: VITAMIN A, VITAMIN C, POTASSIUM, FIBER

INSTRUCTIONS:

1. **Quinoa Chickpea Fusion:** Gently mix the fluffy cooked quinoa with tender chickpeas, juicy cherry tomatoes, and crisp cucumbers in a cozy bowl.
2. **Splash of Sunshine:** Drizzle the vibrant mix with the juice of a fresh lemon, adding a bright and zesty spark.
3. **Cinnamon Surprise:** Dust over a whisper of ground cinnamon, introducing a warm, aromatic twist that's sure to delight.
4. **Blend of Flavors:** Take a moment to thoroughly stir, marrying the diverse flavors into a harmonious salad.
5. **Garnish and Grace:** Before serving, consider a sprinkle of fresh herbs or a light dusting of feta cheese for an added layer of texture and taste.
6. **Ready to Enjoy:** Present this light yet satisfying quinoa and chickpea salad as the perfect centerpiece for a nutritious meal or a refreshing side dish.

31. Chicken and Vegetable Wrap

INGREDIENTS: QUANTITY FOR 1 PERSON

- **Chicken Breast:** 4.41 oz (125g)
- **Whole Wheat Wrap:** 1 medium
- **Lettuce:** 2.21 oz (62.5g)
- **Tomatoes:** 2.21 oz (62.5g)
- **Hummus:** 1.32 oz (37.5g)
- **Ground Cinnamon:** 1/2 teaspoon (1g)

COOKING TIME:

30 minutes

10 minutes

20 minutes

Easy

NUTRITIONAL VALUES (ESTIMATE):

Kcal: ~505 kcal; **CF (Carbohydrates with Fiber):** 0.82 oz (23.3g); **CA (Starchy Carbohydrates):** 1.14 oz (32.5g); **Fats:** 0.44 oz (12.5g); **Proteins:** 0.99 oz (28.1g); **Sodium:** varies depending on the sodium content in hummus and seasonings.

MICRONUTRIENTS: VITAMIN A, VITAMIN C, POTASSIUM, FIBER

INSTRUCTIONS:

1. **Get the chicken just right:** Cook up the chicken breast exactly how you love it, then slice it into whisper-thin strips.
2. **Veggie Time:** Splash some water over the lettuce and tomatoes, getting them fresh and ready.
3. **Setting the Stage:** Unroll that whole wheat wrap and gently spread a layer of creamy hummus all over.
4. **Building Your Masterpiece:** Arrange the tender chicken strips and crisp veggies on the wrap, then sprinkle a hint of cinnamon for a surprising flavor kick.
5. **The Final Twist:** Roll up the wrap carefully, making sure all the delicious filling is snugly enclosed.
6. **Feast Away:** Sit back and savor your scrumptious Chicken and Vegetable Wrap, a true delight in every bite.

32. Barley Salad with Vegetables and Feta

INGREDIENTS: QUANTITY FOR 1 PERSON

- **Cooked Barley:** 7.05 oz (200g)
- **Zucchini:** 3.53 oz (100g)
- **Cherry tomatoes:** 3.53 oz (100g)
- **Feta:** 2.11 oz (60g)
- **Extra Virgin Olive Oil:** 0.71 oz (20g)
- **Chosen Spice:** Ground Cinnamon, 1/2 teaspoon (1g)

COOKING TIME:

15 minutes

10 minutes

5 minutes

Easy

NUTRITIONAL VALUES (ESTIMATE):

Kcal: ~510 kcal; **CF (Carbohydrates with Fiber):** 0.79 oz (22.5g); **CA (Starchy Carbohydrates):** 1.26 oz (35.75g); **Fats:** 0.56 oz (15.75g); **Proteins:** 0.40 oz (11.25g); **Sodium:** varies depending on the sodium content in feta and olive oil.

MICRONUTRIENTS: VITAMIN A, VITAMIN C, FIBER

INSTRUCTIONS:

1. **Barley Basics:** Get the barley going as per the box's say-so. Once it's done, give it a drain and let it chill out.
2. **Veggie Prep:** Turn those zucchinis into cubes and give the cherry tomatoes a rough chop.
3. **Skillet Magic:** Warm up some olive oil in a skillet, toss in the zucchini, and cook it until it's just right.
4. **Tomato Twist:** Throw in the cherry tomatoes and a dash of cinnamon with the zucchini, letting it all mingle for a few.
5. **Mix it Up:** In a big bowl, bring together the barley and your skillet goodies.
6. **Feta Finale:** Crumble in the feta and give it a good stir.
7. **Dish it out:** Serve up your barley salad masterpiece and dig into the goodness.

.33. Salmon Burger

INGREDIENTS: QUANTITY FOR 1 PERSON

- **Ground Salmon:** 5.29 oz (150g)
- **Whole Grain Hamburger Buns:** 1.8 oz, about 2 thin slices (54g)
- **Green Salad:** 2.65 oz, about 1/2 cup (75g)
- **Tomato:** 2.65 oz, about 1/2 cup (75g)
- **Greek Yogurt:** 1.59 oz, about 2 tablespoons (45g)
- **Fresh Grated Ginger:** 0.35 oz, about 1 teaspoon (10g)

COOKING TIME:

	20 minutes
	10 minutes
	10 minutes
	Easy

NUTRITIONAL VALUES (ESTIMATE):

Total Calories: about 481 kcal; **Total Proteins:** 1.64 oz (about 46.5g); **Total Fats:** 0.71 oz (about 20g); **Total Carbohydrates:** 1.27 oz. about 36g; **Carbohydrates with Fiber:** about 0.26 oz (7.5g); **Carbohydrates with Starch:** about 1 oz (28.5g); **Total Sodium:** about 0.001 oz (33.75mg).

MICRONUTRIENTS: VITAMIN A, VITAMIN C, POTASSIUM, FIBER

INSTRUCTIONS:

1. **Start with Salmon:** In a cozy bowl, gently mix the salmon with a hint of ginger to wake up the flavors.
2. **Patty Time:** Mold that salmon mix into a nice patty and cook it in your favorite pan or over the grill until it's perfectly done to your taste.
3. **Bun Prep:** Take a wholesome whole-grain bun and lightly toast it for that perfect crunch.
4. **Zesty Dressing:** Stir together some creamy Greek yogurt with an extra dash of ginger for a kick.
5. **Layering Up:** Lay the juicy salmon patty on the toasted bun's bottom, followed by a fresh layer of greens and a few tomato slices for a burst of freshness.
6. **Top It Off:** Generously spread your zesty Greek yogurt dressing on the bun's top half.
7. **Burger Bliss:** Cap it, press it gently, and take a moment to savor your creation—a burger that's as delicious as it is friendly to your health.

34. Lean Beef Steak with Roasted Vegetables

INGREDIENTS: QUANTITY FOR 1 PERSON

- **Lean Beef Steak:** 4 oz (about 113g)
- **Asparagus:** 3 oz, about 1 cup cut (85g)
- **Red capsicum:** 2 oz, about 1/2 cup strips (57g)
- **Mushrooms:** 2 oz, about 1/2 cup sliced (57g)
- **Extra Virgin Olive Oil:** 1 tablespoon (15ml)
- **Garlic, Minced:** 1 teaspoon (5g)
- **Fresh Rosemary, Chopped:** 1 teaspoon (5g)
- **Sea Salt:** to taste
- **Black Pepper:** to taste

COOKING TIME:

 30 minutes

 10 minutes

20 minutes

Medium

NUTRITIONAL VALUES (ESTIMATE):

Kcal: ~500 kcal; **CF (Carbohydrates with Fiber):** 1.41 oz (40g); **CA (Carbohydrates with Starch):** 0.71 oz (20g); **F (Fats):** 1.06 oz (30g); **P (Proteins):** 1.41 oz (40g); **S (Sodium):** Varies depending on added salt.

MICRONUTRIENTS: VITAMIN A, VITAMIN C, POTASSIUM, FIBER

INSTRUCTIONS:

1. **Veggie Prep:** Give the asparagus, bell peppers, and mushrooms a good rinse. Chop the asparagus, slice the peppers into strips, and chop the mushrooms too.
2. **Steak Seasoning:** Dust the steak with salt, pepper, a bit of minced garlic, and a sprinkle of fresh rosemary.
3. **Prepare the Baking Sheet:** Place a piece of parchment paper on a perforated baking sheet. Arrange the potatoes, drizzle with a bit of olive oil, and if you like, add pepper. If you must use salt, use it sparingly.
4. **Oven Ready:** Heat your oven to 200°C (392°F) and let those veggies roast for 10 minutes.
5. **Steak Time:** Get a skillet hot over medium-high, pop the steak in, and sear it for about 4-5 minutes on each side to hit that medium-sweet spot.
6. **Veggie Flip:** Pull the veggies out, give them a flip, and back in they go for another 10 minutes until they're tender and getting that golden edge.
7. **Plating Up:** Slice that steak and plate it up with a side of those perfectly roasted veggies

35. Barley and Chicken Soup with Turmeric

INGREDIENTS: QUANTITY FOR 1 PERSON

- **Barley:** 3.14 oz, about 1/3 cup (88.75g)
- **Chicken Breast:** 6.23 oz (176.4g)
- **Carrots:** 3.14 oz, about 1/3 cup (88.75g)
- **Celery:** 3.14 oz, about 1/3 cup (88.75g)
- **Chicken Broth:** about 2 1/2 cups, equivalent to 625ml
- **Turmeric:** A beneficial spice for diabetes with antioxidant and anti-inflammatory properties (quantity not specified, add to taste)

COOKING TIME:

Varies depending on the cooking time of barley and chicken.

10 minutes

Varies depending on the cooking time of barley and chicken.

Easy

NUTRITIONAL VALUES (ESTIMATE):

Kcal: about 470 kcal; **CF (Carbohydrates with Fiber):** about 2.77 oz (about 78.6g); **CA (Starchy Carbohydrates):** about 2.62 oz (about 74.4g); **F (Fats):** about 0.07 oz (about 2g); **P (Proteins):** about 1.11 oz (about 31.5g); **S (Sodium):** about 0.024 oz (about 700mg).

MICRONUTRIENTS: VITAMIN A, VITAMIN C, POTASSIUM, FIBER

INSTRUCTIONS:

1. **Warm Up the Broth:** Begin by heating your chicken broth until it's gently boiling.
2. **Prep Your Ingredients:** Take a moment to chop the chicken breast into bite-sized pieces, and dice those carrots and celery into friendly little cubes.
3. **Barley's Turn:** Scatter the barley into the simmering broth, letting it cook until it's tender but still has a bit of bite to it.
4. **Combine and Simmer:** Now, it's time to introduce the chicken, carrots, and celery to the pot. Let everything mingle and cook together until the chicken is thoroughly cooked and the veggies are soft.
5. **Taste and Tweak:** Give your soup a careful taste, adjusting the seasoning with a pinch of salt if needed.
6. **Serve with Warmth:** Dish up this comforting barley and chicken soup, perfect for warming up any meal.

8.3. Dinner

36. Grilled Chicken Breast with Steamed Broccoli and Quinoa

INGREDIENTS: QUANTITY FOR 1 PERSON:

- **Grilled Chicken Breast:** 5.29 oz, (150g)
- **Steamed Broccoli:** 3.53 oz, about 2 cups chopped (100g)
- **Quinoa:** 1.59 oz, about ½ cup (45g)
- **Cherry Tomatoes:** 1.76 oz, about ⅔ cup (50g)
- **Olive Oil (for dressing):** 2 teaspoons (0.35 oz, 10g)
- **Lemon Juice and Herbs for flavoring:** Variable amount

COOKING TIME:

⏱	20 minutes
🍲	10 minutes
🥄	10 minutes
❀	Medium

NUTRITIONAL VALUES (ESTIMATE):

Calories: ~434.5 kcal; **CF (Carbohydrates with Fiber):** 0.16 oz (4.46g); **CA (Starchy Carbohydrates):** 0.64 oz (18.13g); **F (Fats):** 0.59 oz (16.76g); **P (Proteins):** 1.82 oz (51.73g); **S (Sodium):** 0.0052 ounces (148.5 mg).

MICRONUTRIENTS: VITAMIN A, VITAMIN C, POTASSIUM, FIBER

INSTRUCTIONS:

1. **Season the chicken breast:** Before grilling, sprinkle the chicken breast with a bit of olive oil and herbs of choice.
2. Preheat the grill and cook the chicken breast until fully cooked.
3. **Prepare the Broccoli:** Wash the broccoli and steam until tender.
4. **Cook the Quinoa:** Prepare the quinoa according to the package instructions.
5. Prepare the cherry tomatoes. Wash and cut the cherry tomatoes in half.
6. **Season the Quinoa:** In a bowl, mix the cooked quinoa with the cherry tomatoes; add olive oil, lemon juice, and herbs for flavor.
7. **Assemble the dish:** Arrange the grilled chicken breast, steamed broccoli, and quinoa salad on a plate.
8. **Serve:** Enjoy the meal warm or at room temperature, adding more lemon juice or herbs to taste.

37. Grilled Turkey with Steamed Asparagus

INGREDIENTS: QUANTITY FOR 1 PERSON

- **Turkey Breast, skinless:** 5.44 oz, about ⅔ cup (154.13g)
- **Asparagus:** 4.53 oz, about ½ cup (128.44g)
- **Olive Oil:** 0.22 oz, about 2 teaspoons (6.42ml)
- **Lemon Juice:** 0.65 oz, about 3 teaspoons (19.27ml)
- **Garlic Powder:** 0.64 oz, about 3 and ½ teaspoons (3.21ml)
- **Turmeric Powder:** 0.64 oz, about 3 and ½ teaspoons (3.21ml) (Optional)

COOKING TIME:

20 minutes	
10 minutes	
10 minutes	
Easy	

NUTRITIONAL VALUES (ESTIMATE):

Total Calories: 399.99 kcal; **Carbohydrates with Fiber:** 0.26 oz (7.24g); **Starchy Carbohydrates:** 0.24 oz (6.90g); **Fats:** 0.65 oz (18.39g); **Proteins:** 1.68 oz (47.68g); **Sodium:** 4.67 oz (132.29mg).

MICRONUTRIENTS: VITAMIN A, VITAMIN C, POTASSIUM, FIBER

INSTRUCTIONS:

1. **Turkey Seasoning:** Get your turkey breast ready by giving it a rub with garlic powder and turmeric, then add a squeeze of lemon juice for that extra zing.
2. **Grilling Magic:** Heat your grill and let the turkey breast cook until it's perfectly done.
3. **Tender Asparagus:** Wash the asparagus and steam them until they're soft and full of flavor.
4. **Emulsion Creation:** In a small bowl, mix up some olive oil with a dash more of lemon juice until it comes together in a light, tangy dressing.
5. **Dishing Up:** Arrange the beautifully grilled turkey on a plate with the tender asparagus by its side.
6. **Dressing Drizzle:** Spoon over your homemade olive oil and lemon emulsion to bring the dish together with a fresh burst of flavor.

38. Eggplant and Chickpea Stew

INGREDIENTS: QUANTITY FOR 1 PERSON:

- **Eggplant, diced:** 6.40 oz, about 1¼ cups (181.38g)
- **Cooked Chickpeas:** 2.13 oz, about ⅓ cup (60.46g)
- **Diced Tomatoes, canned:** 4.27 oz, about ⅔ cup (120.92g)
- **Onion, chopped:** 2.13 oz, about ⅓ cup (60.46g)
- **Garlic, minced:** 0.43 oz, about 1 teaspoon (12.09g)
- **Olive Oil:** 0.64 oz, about 2 teaspoons (18.14ml)
- **Cumin Powder:** 0.21 oz, about 1 teaspoon (6.05ml)
- **Paprika:** 0.11 oz, about ½ teaspoon (3.02ml)

COOKING TIME:

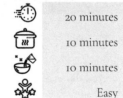

20 minutes	
10 minutes	
10 minutes	
Easy	

NUTRITIONAL VALUES (ESTIMATE):

Kcal: ~385 kcal; **CF (Carbohydrates with Fiber):** 0.50 oz (14.27g); **CA (Starchy Carbohydrates):** 1.59 oz (45.04g); **F (Fats):** 0.78 oz (22.17g); **P (Proteins):** 0.40 oz (11.22g); **S (Sodium):** 1.08 oz (30.59mg).

MICRONUTRIENTS: VITAMIN A, VITAMIN C, POTASSIUM, FIBER

INSTRUCTIONS:

1. **Getting Ready:** Rinse and chop up the eggplant, tomatoes, and onion into bite-sized pieces. Don't forget to mince the garlic.
2. **Oil and Aromatics:** Warm some olive oil in a pot and cook the onion and garlic until they're nicely golden and fragrant.
3. **Veggie Mix:** Toss in the eggplant, chickpeas, and tomatoes, and season with cumin and paprika. Give everything a good stir to make sure the flavors start to meld.
4. **Simmer Time:** Cover the pot and let it all simmer together over a medium flame. You're waiting for the eggplant to get soft and lovely for about 10 minutes.
5. **Final Seasoning:** Crack some pepper over it and give it a taste. You want those eggplants and chickpeas to be just right.
6. **Ready to Eat:** Serve up this hearty stew nice and hot. It's perfect on its own or with a slice of whole wheat bread to soak up all the goodness.

39. Baked Cod with Tomato, Rosemary, and Turmeric

INGREDIENTS: QUANTITY FOR 1 PERSON

- **Cod Fillet:** 5 oz, about 1 cup (141g)
- **Cherry Tomatoes:** 4.52 oz, about ¾ cup (128g)
- **Fresh Basil Leaves:** 0.22 oz, about 3 teaspoons (6.5g)
- **Olive Oil:** 0.22 oz, about 2 teaspoons (6.5ml)
- **Lemon Juice:** 0.68 oz, about 3 teaspoons (19.5ml)
- **Garlic, Minced:** 0.45 oz, about 1 teaspoon (12.8g)
- **Fresh Rosemary, Chopped:** 0.22 oz, about 1 teaspoon (6.5g)
- **Turmeric Powder:** 0.11 oz, about ½ teaspoon (3.2g)

COOKING TIME:

	20 minutes
	10 minutes
	10 minutes
	Easy

NUTRITIONAL VALUES (ESTIMATE):

Kcal: ~402 kcal; **CF (Carbohydrates with Fiber):**.52 oz (14.80g); **CA (Starchy Carbohydrates):** 1.75 oz (49.60g); **F (Fats):** 0.79 oz (22.40g); **P (Proteins):** 0.99 oz (28.00g); **S (Sodium):** 1.48 oz (42.00mg).

MICRONUTRIENTS: VITAMIN A, VITAMIN C, POTASSIUM, FIBER

INSTRUCTIONS:

1. **Get Set:** Fire up your oven to 180°C (356°F). Split the cherry tomatoes, dice the garlic and rosemary, and gently tear the basil leaves.
2. **Cod Seasoning:** Lay the cod in a baking dish and sprinkle it with the garlic, rosemary, a touch of turmeric, a squeeze of lemon, and a splash of olive oil.
3. **Tomato Time:** Scatter the halved tomatoes around the cod.
4. **Into the oven:** Pop the dish in the oven for about 10 minutes, until the cod is just right and flaky.
5. **Basil Finish:** Sprinkle the cooked cod with those hand-torn basil leaves for a fresh touch.
6. **Ready to Enjoy:** Serve it up warm, ready to delight.

40. Chicken stuffed with Spinach and Feta

INGREDIENTS: QUANTITY FOR 1 PERSON

- **Chicken Breast, skinless:** 4.90 oz, about 1 cup (138.82g)
- **Spinach, cooked and squeezed dry:** 2.86 oz, about ½ cup (80.98g)
- **Feta Cheese:** 1.22 oz, about ¼ cup (34.70g)
- **Olive Oil:** 0.20 oz, about 1 teaspoon (5.78ml)
- **Garlic Powder:** 0.10 oz, about ½ teaspoon (2.89ml)

COOKING TIME:

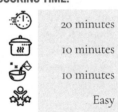

	20 minutes
	10 minutes
	10 minutes
	Easy

NUTRITIONAL VALUES (ESTIMATE):

Kcal: ~388 kcal; **CF (Carbohydrates with Fiber):** 0.06 oz (1.79g); **CA (Starchy Carbohydrates):** 0.13 oz (3.70g); **F (Fats):** 0.65 oz (18.41g); **P (Proteins):** 1.79 oz (50.72g); **S (Sodium):** 0.0187 oz (529.18mg).

MICRONUTRIENTS: VITAMIN A, VITAMIN C, POTASSIUM, FIBER

INSTRUCTIONS:

1. **Preparing the Chicken:** Butterfly the skinless chicken breast and sprinkle the inside with garlic powder.
2. **Preparing the Filling:** In a bowl, mix the cooked spinach with crumbled feta cheese.
3. **Stuffing the Chicken:** Fill the chicken breast with the spinach and feta mixture, then secure it with toothpicks.
4. **Cooking:** Preheat the oven to 180°C (356°F). Lightly grease the chicken with olive oil and place it on a baking tray.
5. **Bake the stuffed chicken:** and let it brown for about a quarter of an hour until it is perfectly cooked.
6. **To serve:** Remove the toothpicks and bring the chicken to the table while it's still hot, cutting it into slices if you prefer.

41. Stir-Fried Tofu and Vegetables

INGREDIENTS: QUANTITY FOR 1 PERSON:

- **Firm Tofu:** 5.64 ounces (160g)
- **Broccoli, florets:** 2.82 ounces (80g)
- **Carrots, sliced:** 2.82 ounces (80g)
- **Bell Pepper, sliced:** 2.82 ounces (80g)
- **Soysauce (low sodium):** 1.06 ounces (30g)
- **Sesame Oil:** 0.18 ounce (5g)
- **Ginger, grated:** 0.71 ounce (20g)
- **Garlic, minced:** 0.71 ounce (20g)
- **Ground Cinnamon:** 1/2 teaspoon (2.5ml)

COOKING TIME:

⏱	20 minutes
🍲	10 minutes
🥣	10 minutes
❄	Easy

NUTRITIONAL VALUES (ESTIMATE):

Kcal: ~397 kcal; **CF (Carbohydrates with Fiber):** 0.33 ounce (9.44g); **CA (Starchy Carbohydrates):** 0.67 ounce (18.96g); **F (Fats):** 0.72 ounce (20.56g); **P (Proteins):** 0.45 ounce (12.88g); **S (Sodium):** 0.0064 ounce (180.2mg).

MICRONUTRIENTS: VITAMIN A, VITAMIN C, POTASSIUM,

INSTRUCTIONS:

1. **Start with Oil:** Warm up some sesame oil in a non-stick skillet.
2. **Aromatic Base:** Toss in the minced garlic and grated ginger, sautéing until they release their inviting aromas.
3. **Veggie Stir-Fry:** Add the broccoli, carrots, and bell pepper into the mix, frying them up until they're just tender yet still have a bit of bite.
4. **Tofu Time:** Drop in the tofu cubes, stirring gently as they warm up and soak in the flavors, for a few minutes.
5. **Soy Sauce Splash:** Drizzle the mix with low-sodium soy sauce, ensuring everything gets a nice coating.
6. **Cinnamon Spark:** Sprinkle a bit of ground cinnamon over the top for that unexpected flavor twist, and give it a good stir.
7. **Ready to Dish:** Serve everything up hot and ready to enjoy.

42. Turkey and Vegetable Skillet

INGREDIENTS: QUANTITY FOR 1 PERSON

- **Lean Ground Turkey (95% lean):** 6.66 ounces (189.72g)
- **Zucchini, diced:** 3.33 ounces (94.86g)
- **Red capsicum, diced:** 3.33 ounces (94.86g)
- **Onion, diced:** 1.66 ounces (47.43g)
- **Olive Oil:** 0.27 ounce (7.72g)
- **Herbs:** 0.14 ounce (4.02g)

COOKING TIME:

⏱	20 minutes
🍲	10 minutes
🥣	10 minutes
❄	Easy

NUTRITIONAL VALUES (ESTIMATE):

Kcal: ~400 kcal; **CF (Carbohydrates with Fiber):** 0.37 ounce (10.62g); **CA (Starchy Carbohydrates):** 0.67 ounce (18.96g); **F (Fats):** 0.72 ounce (20.56g); **P (Proteins):** 0.98 ounce (27.66g); **S (Sodium):** 0.0047 ounce (132.80 mg).

MICRONUTRIENTS: VITAMIN A, VITAMIN C, POTASSIUM,

INSTRUCTIONS:

1. **Warm Up the Skillet:** Get your non-stick skillet nice and hot over a medium-high flame.
2. **Olive Oil Time:** Swirl some olive oil into the skillet, letting it get warm for a quick minute.
3. **Onion and Herbs:** Toss in the chopped onions and a sprinkle of Italian herbs, sautéing until everything's smelling wonderful and the onions are clear.
4. **Turkey Addition:** Crumble the ground turkey into the skillet, stirring and cooking until it's completely browned and cooked.
5. **Veggies Join in:** Mix in the zucchini and red bell pepper, combining them well with the turkey mixture. Cook until the veggies are just soft.
6. **Ready to Serve:** Take it off the heat and serve your skillet creation steaming hot.

43. Stir-Fried Beef and Broccoli

INGREDIENTS: QUANTITY FOR 1 PERSON

- **Lean beef, sliced:** 3.62 oz, about ¼ cup (102.72g)
- **Broccoli florets:** 5.44 oz, about ⅓ cup (154.08g)
- **Low-sodium soy sauce:** 0.54 oz, about 1 tablespoon (15.41g)
- **Sesame oil:** 0.18 oz, about 1 teaspoon (5.14g)
- **Garlic, minced:** 0.36 oz, about 1 teaspoon (10.27g)
- **Ginger, grated:** 0.36 oz, about 1 teaspoon (10.27g)
- **Cornstarch:** 0.18 oz, about 1 teaspoon (5.14g)

COOKING TIME:

⏱	20 minutes
🍲	10 minutes
🥣	10 minutes
❄	Medium

NUTRITIONAL VALUES (ESTIMATE):

Kcal: 400 kcal; **CF (Carbohydrates with Fiber):** 0.72 oz (20.27g); **CA (Starchy Carbohydrates):** 0.165 oz (4.67g); **F (Fats):** 0.75 oz (21.30g); **P (Proteins):** 1.13 oz (32.17g); **S (Sodium):** 0.0048 ounces (0.136 g).

MICRONUTRIENTS: VITAMIN A, VITAMIN C, POTASSIUM, FIBER.

INSTRUCTIONS:

1. **Skillet Prep:** Start by getting your skillet good and hot on a medium-high setting.
2. **Oil in the Pan:** Next, add a good glug of olive oil and let it heat up for a moment.
3. **Sauté Onions and Herbs:** Throw in the onions and a generous shake of Italian herbs. Stir them around until the onions are soft and the air is filled with the scent of herbs.
4. **Ground Turkey Time:** Crumble the ground turkey into the pan. Use a wooden spoon to break it up and stir until it's evenly browned and cooked all the way through.
5. **Add in the Greens:** Now, introduce the zucchini and red bell peppers to the mix, stirring them into the turkey. Let everything cook together until the veggies are just the right amount of tender.
6. **Dish It Out:** Once everything is perfectly cooked, remove it from the heat, and it's ready to dish up, nice and hot.
7. **Garnish and Enjoy:** For a final touch, maybe sprinkle a little fresh parsley on top for color and freshness before serving.

44. Grilled Vegetable Salad with Quinoa

INGREDIENTS: QUANTITY FOR 1 PERSON

- **Cooked quinoa:** 3.50 oz, about ⅔ cup (99.27g)
- **Zucchini, sliced:** 7.00 oz, about 1⅓ cup (198.53g)
- **Eggplant, sliced:** 7.00 oz, about 1⅓ cup (198.53g)
- **Red bell pepper, sliced:** 3.50 oz, about ⅔ cup (99.27g)
- **Olive oil:** 0.35 oz, about 1 teaspoon (9.99g)
- **Balsamic vinegar:** 1.05 oz, about 2 teaspoons (29.78g)
- **Fresh basil, chopped:** 0.35 oz, about 1 teaspoon (9.93g)

COOKING TIME:

30 minutes

20 minutes

10 minutes

Easy

NUTRITIONAL VALUES (ESTIMATE):

Kcal: ~350 kcal; **CF (Carbohydrates with Fiber):** 1.76 oz (50.00g); **F (Fats):** 0.47 oz (13.33g); **P (Proteins):** 0.33 oz (9.40g); **S (Sodium):** 0.70 oz (19.75g).

MICRONUTRIENTS: VITAMIN A, VITAMIN C, POTASSIUM,

INSTRUCTIONS:

1. **Quinoa Time:** Start by cooking the quinoa just like the package suggests. Once it's fluffy and done, put it aside for now.
2. **Grill Gets Hot:** Fire up your grill, or if you're using a grill pan, get that heating. While it's warming, slice up your zucchini, eggplant, and red bell pepper into nice, grill-friendly pieces.
3. **Veggie Prep:** Give those slices a light coat of olive oil, just enough to make them sizzle on the grill.
4. **Veggie Grillin':** Lay your veggies on the grill, watching as they get those beautiful char marks and become perfectly tender.
5. **Dressing Magic:** Grab a bowl and whisk together some olive oil, balsamic vinegar, and a handful of freshly chopped basil for a dressing that's bursting with flavor.
6. **Salad Assembly:** Toss the fluffy quinoa and those gorgeous grilled veggies into a large salad bowl.
7. **Dress It Up:** Drizzle your homemade dressing over the salad, giving it a good mix to make sure every bite is flavorful.
8. **Enjoy:** Plate up your grilled vegetable and quinoa salad, ready to dive into a meal that's as delicious as it is wholesome.

45. Grilled Salmon and Avocado Salad

INGREDIENTS: QUANTITY FOR 1 PERSON

- **Grilled Salmon:** 3.70 oz (105.01g)
- **Avocado:** 1.48 oz, about ⅓ cup (42.01g)
- **Mixed Greens:** 1.85 oz, about 3 cups (52.51g)
- **Cherry Tomatoes:** 1.11 oz, about ¾ cup (31.50g)
- **Cucumbers:** 1.85 oz, about ¾ cup (52.51g)
- **Extra Virgin Olive Oil and Balsamic Vinegar:** 0.37 oz, about 2 teaspoons (10.50g)

COOKING TIME:

20 minutes

10 minutes

10 minutes

Easy

NUTRITIONAL VALUES (ESTIMATE):

Kcal: ~400 kcal; **CF (Carbohydrates with Fiber):** 0.25 oz (7.19g); **CA (Carbohydrates Starches):** Not applicable, as carbs are mainly from fiber; **F (Fats):** 1.08 oz (30.68g); **P (Proteins):** 0.81 oz (22.99g); **S (Sodium):** 0.0029 oz (82.96mg);

INSTRUCTIONS:

1. **Salmon Seasoning:** Lightly season the salmon fillet with salt and pepper to taste before it hits the grill.
2. **Grilling Time:** Fire up the grill and cook the salmon until it's just right and flaky.
3. **Salad Prep:** Give the mixed greens a good rinse and pat them dry.
4. **Avocado & Tomatoes:** Slice the avocado neatly and halve those juicy cherry tomatoes.
5. **Cucumber Slices:** Clean and slice the cucumbers nice and thin.
6. **Dressing Mix:** Whisk together some olive oil and balsamic vinegar in a small bowl for the dressing.
7. **Salad Assembly:** Toss the greens, grilled salmon, avocado slices, cherry tomatoes, and cucumber slices in a big salad bowl.
8. **Adding the Dressing:** Drizzle your dressing over the salad, giving it a light toss to coat everything evenly..
9. **Ready to Serve:** Plate your salad and dive into the freshness and burst of flavors.;

46. Chicken and Mushroom Soup

INGREDIENTS: QUANTITY FOR 1 PERSON

- **Diced Chicken Breast:** 3.53 Oz, about ½ cup (100g)
- **Sliced Mushrooms:** 3.53 oz, about 1 cup (100g)
- **Low-Sodium Chicken Broth:** 17.59 oz, about 2 cups (500ml)
- **Diced Onion:** 1.76 oz, about ½ cup (50g)
- **Minced Garlic:** 0.35 oz, about 2 teaspoons (10g); Thyme: 1 teaspoon (5ml).
- **Olive Oil:** 1 teaspoon (5ml)

COOKING TIME:

30 minutes

10 minutes

20 minutes.

NUTRITIONAL VALUES (ESTIMATE):

Total Calories: 246.9 kcal; **Proteins:** 1.33 oz (37.79g); **Fats:** 0.18 oz (5.00g); **Total Carbohydrates (with starch):** 0.47 oz (13.25g); **Fiber:** 0.07 oz (2.06g); **Sodium:** 0.01 oz (282.7mg).

MICRONUTRIENTS: VITAMIN C, POTASSIUM, FIBER, AND OTHER MINERALS FROM MUSHROOMS AND CHICKEN BROTH

INSTRUCTIONS:

1. Get the chicken and mushrooms ready. Chop up the chicken breast and mushrooms into bite-sized pieces.
2. **Start with the basics:** Warm up some olive oil in a pot and gently cook the onion and garlic until they're soft and fragrant.
3. **Brown the Goodies:** Toss in the chicken and mushrooms, cooking until they get a nice golden color.
4. **Broth Time:** Add the chicken broth and sprinkle in some thyme for that herby goodness.
5. **Let It Simmer:** Bring everything to a lively boil, then turn down the heat and let it all simmer together, giving the chicken time to cook through.
6. **Soup's Up:** Ladle the soup into bowls hot, tweaking the seasoning with a bit more salt if needed and maybe a sprinkle of fresh thyme on top for flair.

47. Steamed Turkey Meatballs with Vegetables

INGREDIENTS: QUANTITY FOR 1 PERSON

- **Lean Ground Turkey:** 4.42 oz, about ½ cup (125.43g)
- **Carrots:** 2.21 oz, about ⅓ cup (62.72g)
- **Zucchini:** 2.21 oz, about ⅓ cup (62.72g)
- **Low-Sodium Soy Sauce:** 1.27 tablespoons (18.81ml)
- **Garlic:** 2.54 teaspoons (12.54g)
- **Onion:** 1.33 oz, about ¼ cup (37.63g)
- **Olive Oil:** 1.27 teaspoons (6.27ml)
- **Herbs of Choice:** Variable quantity

COOKING TIME:

⏱	30 minutes
🍲	15 minutes
🥄	15 minutes
❄	Medium

NUTRITIONAL VALUES (ESTIMATE):

Calories: ~400 kcal; **CF (Carbohydrates with Fiber):** 0.55 oz (15.60g); **CA (Starchy Carbohydrates):** 0.43 oz (12.32g); **F (Fats):** 0.32 oz (9.19g); **P (Proteins):** 1.15 oz (32.64g); **S (Sodium):** 0.03 oz (863.47mg).

MICRONUTRIENTS: VITAMIN A (FROM CARROTS), VITAMIN C (FROM ZUCCHINI), POTASSIUM, FIBER

INSTRUCTIONS:

1. **Getting the Meatballs Ready:** Combine ground turkey, finely chopped onion, garlic, a mix of herbs, and a splash of soy sauce.
2. **Shaping the Meatballs:** Roll the turkey blend into small, bite-sized meatballs.
3. **Steam to Perfection:** Cook the meatballs in a steamer until they're thoroughly done.
4. **Veggie Time:** While those are steaming, either steam or lightly sauté carrots and zucchini, adding just a touch of olive oil for flavor.
5. **Bringing It Together:** Plate the juicy turkey meatballs alongside the tender vegetables.
6. **Final Touch:** Drizzle a little more soy sauce over the dish before serving, to taste.

48. Baked Cod with Olives and Cherry Tomatoes

INGREDIENTS: QUANTITY FOR 1 PERSON

- **Cod Fillet:** 5.98 oz, (169.54g)
- **Cherry Tomatoes:** 1.99 oz, about ⅔ cup (56.51g)
- **Black Olives, pitted:** 1.20 oz, about ⅓ cup (33.91g)
- **Garlic:** 2.29 teaspoons (11.30g)
- **Olive Oil:** 1.15 tablespoons (16.95ml)
- **Lemon juice:** 1.15 tablespoons (16.95ml)
- **Oregano:** 1 teaspoon (5ml)

COOKING TIME:

⏱	25 minutes
🍲	10 minutes
🥄	15 minutes
❄	Easy

NUTRITIONAL VALUES (ESTIMATE):

Calories: ~400 kcal; **CF (Carbohydrates with Fiber):** 0.32 oz (9.14g); **CA (Starchy Carbohydrates):** 0.28 oz (8.05g); **F (Fats):** 0.80 oz (22.55g); **P (Proteins):** 1.43 oz (40.50g); **S (Sodium):** 0.01 oz (383.39mg).

MICRONUTRIENTS: VITAMIN A, VITAMIN C, POTASSIUM, FIBER

INSTRUCTIONS:

1. **Cod Prep:** Give the cod a nice rub with lemon juice, a bit of chopped garlic, and a sprinkle of oregano.
2. **Tomatoes and Olives:** Scatter some cherry tomatoes and olives around the cod in a baking dish.
3. **Olive Oil Touch:** Give everything a good drizzle of olive oil for flavor.
4. **Oven Time:** Heat your oven and let the cod bake at 356°F (180°C) for 15 minutes or until it's perfectly cooked through.
5. **Ready to Enjoy:** Dish out the cod hot, maybe with a little extra oregano on top for a fresh burst.

49. Vegetable and Lentil Soup

INGREDIENTS: QUANTITY FOR 1 PERSON

- **Lentils:** 2.77 oz, about 0.41 cup (78g)
- **Carrots:** 2.77 oz, about 0.6 cups (78g)
- **Celery:** 2.77 oz, about 0.78 cups (78g)
- **Onion:** 2.77 oz, about 0.52 cups (78g)
- **Vegetable Broth:** 27.67 oz, about 3.27 cups (784g)
- **Canned Tomatoes:** 5.53 oz, about 0.65 cups (157g)
- **Garlic:** 0.55 oz, about 0.1 cups (16g)
- **Rosemary:** 0.28 oz, about 0.13 cups (8g)

COOKING TIME:

⏱	30 minutes
🍲	10 minutes
🥣	20 minutes
❄	Easy

NUTRITIONAL VALUES (ESTIMATE):

Kcal: ~400 kcal; **CF (Carbohydrates with Fiber):** 2.82 oz (79.97g); **F (Fats):** 0.19 oz (5.39g); **P (Proteins):** 0.7 oz (19.84g); **S (Sodium):** 115.33 oz (3268.9g).

INSTRUCTIONS:

1. **Kick-off with the prep:** Start your culinary adventure by giving those lentils a nice rinse. Then, grab your veggies—carrots, celery, and onion—and chop them into bite-sized morsels. The garlic? Chop it till it's almost gone.
2. **Veggie Sauté Magic:** In a large pot, let a drizzle of olive oil heat up over a medium flame. Add your prepped veggies and stir them around until they begin to soften and fill the kitchen with their inviting aroma.
3. **Lentils Join the Party:** With the veggies ready, toss in the lentils, along with the tomatoes and a few rosemary sprigs for that herbaceous kick.; **The Broth Transformation:** Next, pour in the vegetable broth and watch the magic happen. Bring it to a boil, then simmer down and wait for the lentils to get perfectly tender—about 20 minutes should do the trick.
4. **Seasoning Finale:** Give it a taste and tweak the seasoning with salt and pepper to get it just how you like it.
5. **Serving Time:** Once it's all hot and ready, ladle your masterpiece into bowls. Pair it with a slice of whole-wheat bread for the ultimate comfort meal. Enjoy the fruits of your labor, served with a side of warmth and satisfaction.

50. Ratatouille with Polenta

INGREDIENTS: QUANTITY FOR 1 PERSON:

- **Cooked Polenta:** 3.98 oz, about 0.68 cups (113g).
- **Eggplant:** 2.84 oz, about 0.58 cups (81g)
- **Zucchini:** 2.84 oz, about 0.65 cups (81g)
- **Bell Peppers:** 2.84 oz, about 0.54 cups (81g)
- **Tomatoes:** 2.84 oz, about 0.45 cup (81g)
- **Garlic:** 0.57 oz, about 0.11 cups (16g).
- **Olive Oil:** 0.85 oz, about 1.63 tablespoons (24g)
- **Basil:** 0.28 oz, about 3.22 teaspoons (8g)

COOKING TIME:

40 minutes

15 minutes

25 minutes

Medium

NUTRITIONAL VALUES (ESTIMATE):

Kcal: ~399 kcal; **CF (Carbohydrates with Fiber):** 1.44 oz (40.86g); **F (Fats):** 0.9 oz (25.51g); **P (Proteins):** 0.25 oz (7.09g).

MICRONUTRIENTS: VITAMIN A, VITAMIN C, POTASSIUM, FIBER

INSTRUCTIONS:

1. **Start with the veggies:** Begin by washing and cutting the eggplants, zucchinis, bell peppers, and tomatoes into small pieces. Don't forget to finely chop the garlic too.
2. **Polenta Time:** Cook the polenta according to the package directions until it becomes soft and has a creamy texture.
3. **Golden Garlic:** Warm up some olive oil in a big skillet and fry the garlic till it turns a lovely golden color.
4. **Veggie Mix:** Throw in the eggplants, zucchinis, bell peppers, and tomatoes into the skillet. Let them cook on a medium flame, giving them an occasional stir.
5. **Flavor It Up:** Sprinkle in some chopped basil and your favorite spices to taste. Keep cooking until all the vegetables feel just right—nice and tender.
6. **Plating Up:** Spoon out the polenta onto plates and heap the warm ratatouille on top.
7. **Final Touch:** Sprinkle some fresh basil over the top for that extra burst of flavor before you dig in.

51. Lemon and Thyme Chicken with Steamed Vegetables

INGREDIENTS: QUANTITY FOR 1 PERSON:

- **Skinless Chicken Breast:** 5.27 oz, about 0.67 cups (150g)
- **Broccoli Florets:** 4.4 oz, about 1.37 cups (125g)
- **Sliced Carrots:** 2.2 oz, about 0.51 cups (62g)
- **Lemon juice:** 0.66 oz, about 1.26 tablespoons (19g)
- **Fresh Thyme:** 0.22 oz, about 2.49 teaspoons (6g)
- **Minced Garlic:** 0.44 oz, about 0.08 cups (12g)
- **Olive Oil:** 0.22 oz, about 0.42 tablespoons (6g)

COOKING TIME:

	30 minutes
	10 minutes
	20 minutes
	Medium

NUTRITIONAL VALUES (ESTIMATE):

Calories: ~398 kcal; **Carbohydrates with Fiber:** 0.76 oz (21.53g); **Fats:** 0.43 oz (12.17g); **Proteins:** 1.83 oz (51.92g).

MICRONUTRIENTS: VITAMIN A, VITAMIN C, POTASSIUM, FIBER

INSTRUCTIONS:

1. **Flavor the Chicken:** Get the chicken ready by rubbing it with minced garlic, a sprinkle of fresh thyme, and a dash of lemon juice for zest.
2. **Sizzle the chicken:** Pop it into a non-stick skillet with some olive oil. Cook it through, flipping it halfway to make sure it cooks evenly on both sides.
3. **Veggie Prep:** Give the broccoli and carrots a good rinse. Chop the carrots into neat little circles.
4. **Veggie Steam:** Use a steamer to cook the broccoli and carrot slices until they're just the right mix of tender and crunchy.
5. **Dish Assembly:** Slice up the chicken and lay it out on a plate, nestling the steamed veggies alongside. Add a final drizzle of lemon juice and a sprinkle of thyme for extra flair.
6. **Extra Touch:** For those feeling fancy, a side of whole-grain bread or a fresh salad can round out this meal beautifully.

52. Chickpea and Grilled Vegetable Salad

INGREDIENTS: QUANTITY FOR 1 PERSON:

- **Cooked Chickpeas:** 3.22 oz, about 0.38 cups (91g)
- **Bell Peppers:** 2.3 oz, about 0.44 cups (65g)
- **Zucchini:** 2.3 oz, about 0.53 cups (65g)
- **Red Onion:** 1.38 oz, about 0.26 cups (39g)
- **Olive Oil:** 0.69 oz, about 1.32 tablespoons (20g)
- **Balsamic Vinegar:** 0.69 oz, about 1.32 tablespoons (20g)
- **Oregano:** 0.23 oz, about 2.61 teaspoons (7g)

COOKING TIME:

	30 minutes
	15 minutes
	15 minutes
	Easy

NUTRITIONAL VALUES (ESTIMATE):

Calories: ~405 kcal; **Carbohydrates with Fiber:** 1.48 oz (41.95g); **Fats:** 0.81 oz (22.98g); **Proteins:** 0.37 oz (10.49g).

MICRONUTRIENTS: VITAMIN A, VITAMIN C, POTASSIUM, FIBER

INSTRUCTIONS:

1. **Get the Chickpeas Ready:** Either cook up some chickpeas beforehand or use a can of them to save time.
2. **Grill the veggies:** lightly char bell peppers, zucchini, and red onion on the grill until they're just right—a little bit of char but still with a crunch.
3. **Make the dressing:** Stir together some olive oil, balsamic vinegar, and a dash of oregano in a cup for a tasty dressing.
4. **Toss Together:** In your favorite salad bowl, mix the chickpeas with the grilled veggies.
5. **Add the Final Touch:** Pour your dressing over the salad, making sure everything gets a nice coating.
6. **Serve and enjoy:** Your vibrant, nutrient-packed salad is ready to hit the table. Perfect for a refreshing meal.

53. Minestrone with Barley and Vegetables

INGREDIENTS: QUANTITY FOR 1 PERSON:

- **Pearled Barley:** 2.37 oz, about 0.34 cups (67g)
- **Carrots:** 2.37 oz, about 0.55 cups (67g)
- **Zucchini:** 2.37 oz, about 0.54 cups (67g)
- **Cooked Cannellini Beans:** 2.37 oz, about 0.28 cups (67g)
- **Canned Tomatoes:** 4.75 oz, about 0.56 cups (135g)
- **Vegetable Broth:** 23.75 oz, about 2.81 cups (673g)
- **Garlic:** 0.47 oz, about 0.09 cups (13g)
- **Basil:** 0.24 oz, about 2.69 teaspoons (7g)

COOKING TIME:

40 minutes
10 minutes
30 minutes
Medium

NUTRITIONAL VALUES (ESTIMATE):

Calories: ~398 kcal; **Carbohydrates with Fiber:** 2.9 oz (82.21g); **Fats:** 0.17 oz (4.81g); **Proteins:** 0.63 oz (17.86g).

MICRONUTRIENTS: VITAMIN A, VITAMIN C, POTASSIUM, FIBER

INSTRUCTIONS:

1. **Starting with Barley:** Kick things off by cooking the pearled barley just like the packet says.
2. **Veggie Time:** Dice those carrots and zucchini into nice little cubes, and chop the garlic until it's super fine.
3. **Sauté Magic:** In a large pot, warm up a bit of oil and give the garlic a quick fry till it's just turning golden. Then, pile in the carrots, zucchini, cannellini beans, and canned tomatoes with all their juices.
4. **Broth Action:** Pour the veggie broth into the mix and turn up the heat to get a lively boil going.
5. **Barley Joining the Party:** Add your already cooked barley into the pot, mixing it into the lively veggie dance.
6. **Flavor Boost:** Sprinkle in some chopped basil and whatever herbs you love, giving the pot a good stir for that herby goodness.
7. **Let It Bubble:** Turn down the heat and let everything simmer gently, cooking until each veggie is tender to the bite.
8. **Serve It Up:** Now it's time to ladle out your rich, comforting minestrone soup, ready to warm the soul and fill the belly with joy.

54. Spinach and Mushroom Frittata

INGREDIENTS: QUANTITY FOR 1 PERSON:

- **Eggs:** 6.19 oz, about 3.51 cups (176g)
- **Fresh Spinach:** 3.1 oz, about 2.93 cups (88g)
- **Mushrooms:** 3.1 oz, about 1.25 cups (88g)
- **Onion:** 1.86 oz, about 0.35 cups (53g)
- **Skim Milk:** 0.93 oz, about 0.11 cups (26g)
- **Olive Oil:** 0.31 oz, about 0.59 tablespoons (9g)
- **Nutmeg:** 0.01 oz, about 0.16 teaspoons (0g)

COOKING TIME:

25 minutes
10 minutes
15 minutes
Medium

NUTRITIONAL VALUES (ESTIMATE):

Calories: ~401 kcal; **Carbohydrates with Fiber:** 0.48 oz (13.60g); **Fats:** 0.93 oz (26.40g); **Proteins:** 1.02 oz (28.91g).

MICRONUTRIENTS: VITAMIN A, VITAMIN C, POTASSIUM, FIBER

INSTRUCTIONS:

1. **Mixing It Up:** In a bowl, whisk together eggs and a splash of skim milk, and season with a little salt and a sprinkle of nutmeg.
2. **Sauté the Greens and Shrooms:** In a skillet with a drizzle of olive oil, cook the onions and mushrooms until they're tender. Then, add the spinach, letting it wilt and blend in beautifully.
3. **Egg Pour-Over:** Once your veggies look good, evenly pour the egg mix over them in the skillet.
4. **Gentle Cooking:** Turn the heat down to medium-low. Patiently cook the frittata, watching as the edges solidify while the center stays slightly creamy.
5. **Add Cheese:** Sprinkle some grated cheese over the top for an extra layer of flavor. Let it melt into the frittata.
6. **Broil for Perfection:** For a golden finish, pop the skillet under the broiler for a minute or two, just until the top gets a light golden crust.
7. **Serve Warm:** Cut the frittata into wedges and serve it piping hot. Enjoy the melt-in-your-mouth goodness!

55. Chicken and Vegetable Skewers

INGREDIENTS: QUANTITY FOR 1 PERSON:

- **Chicken Breast, cubed:** 3.98 oz, about 0.5 cups (113g)
- **Bell Peppers, cubed:** 1.99 oz, about 0.38 cups (56g)
- **Onion, cubed:** 1.99 oz, about 0.38 cups (56g)
- **Zucchini, cubed:** 1.99 oz, about 0.45 cups (56g)
- **Olive Oil:** 0.6 oz, about 1.14 tablespoons (17g)
- **Lemon juice:** 0.6 oz, about 1.14 tablespoons (17g)
- **Paprika:** 0.2 oz, about 2.45 teaspoons (6g)

COOKING TIME:

	30 minutes
	15 minutes
	15 minutes
	Medium

NUTRITIONAL VALUES (ESTIMATE):

Calories: ~402 kcal; **Carbohydrates with Fiber:** 0.51 oz (14.45g); **Fats:** 0.78 oz (22.06g); **Proteins:** 1.33 oz (37.74g); **Sodium:** 3.41 oz (96.65g).

MICRONUTRIENTS: VITAMIN A, VITAMIN C, POTASSIUM, FIBER

INSTRUCTIONS:

1. **Let's prepare everything:** take a cutting board and a knife and chop the chicken, onion, zucchini, and bell pepper into small pieces.
2. **Flavor the Chicken:** Combine the chicken pieces in a bowl with some oil and lemon, and a sprinkle of paprika to taste.
3. **Skewer Time:** Skewer the chicken and veggies, alternating them for a colorful mix.
4. **Grill to Perfection:** Fire up the grill or grill pan and cook the skewers, turning them now and then, until the chicken is fully done and the veggies have those perfect grill marks.
5. **Dish It Out:** Plate the hot skewers with a side salad or some whole grain bread for a complete meal.
6. **Marinate for Flavor:** Let the chicken marinate in the seasoning mix for at least 30 minutes before skewering to enhance the flavors.
7. **Final Touch:** Enjoy your meal!

8.4. Snack

56. Oat and Blueberry Mini Muffins

INGREDIENTS: QUANTITY FOR 1 PERSON

- **Oat Flakes (CF):** about 1/3 oz, 1 tablespoon (10g)
- **Fresh Blueberries (CF):** about 0.1 oz, less than 1 tablespoon (3g)
- **Egg (P):** 1
- **Ground Almonds (F, P):** about 0.07 oz, about 1/2 teaspoon (2g)
- **Low-Fat Greek Yogurt (P, F):** about 0.7 oz, about 1 tablespoon (20g)
- **Mashed Banana (CF):** about 0.35 oz, about 1 tablespoon (10g)
- **Ground Flaxseeds (CF, F, P):** about 0.1 oz, about 1/2 teaspoon (3g)
- **Honey (CF):** about 0.07 oz, less than 1/2 teaspoon (2g)
- **Grilled Chicken Breast (P):** about 1.41 oz (40g)
- **Fresh Spinach (CF):** about 1.06 oz, about 1 cup (30g)

COOKING TIME:

	40 minutes
	20 minutes
	20 minutes
	Medium

NUTRITIONAL VALUES (PER SERVING):

Calories: 150 kcal; **CF:** about 0.53 oz (15g); **CA:** about 0.18 oz (5g); **F:** about 0.18 oz (5g); **P:** about 0.32 oz (9g).

MICRONUTRIENTS: VITAMIN C, VITAMIN E, POTASSIUM, FIBER

INSTRUCTIONS:

1. **1 Warm Up:** Turn your oven on to 180°C (350°F) to get it nice and hot.
2. **Mix the Batter:** Grab a bowl and toss in oat flakes, fresh blueberries, an egg, some ground almonds, low-fat Greek yogurt, a mashed banana, ground flaxseeds, and a bit of honey. Stir it all up.
3. **Muffin Time:** Spoon that tasty batter into mini muffin molds and pop them in the oven. Bake for 15-20 minutes until they're looking golden and delicious.
4. **Chicken Prep:** While those muffins are baking, grill a chicken breast, then cut it into small pieces.
5. **Spinach Ready:** Give the spinach a good rinse and chop it up if the leaves are too big.
6. **Plate It:** Time to put it all together. Arrange those warm mini muffins, juicy grilled chicken, and fresh spinach on a plate.
7. **Extra Flair:** If you're feeling fancy, drizzle some extra virgin olive oil over the spinach and sprinkle a little salt and pepper on top to taste.

57. Greek Yogurt with Nuts and Fruit

INGREDIENTS: QUANTITY FOR 1 PERSON

- **Low-Fat Greek Yogurt:** 3.17 oz, about ½ cup (90g)
- **Chopped Nuts:** 0.32 oz, about 2 teaspoons (9g)
- **Blueberries:** 0.32 oz, less than ¼ cup (9g)
- **Sliced Banana:** 0.63 oz, about 1½ tablespoons (18g)
- **Chia Seeds:** 0.32 oz, about 2 teaspoons (9g)
- **Honey:** 0.32 oz, about 2 teaspoons (9g)

COOKING TIME:

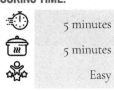

5 minutes

5 minutes

Easy

NUTRITIONAL VALUES (ESTIMATE):

Calories: 204.21 kcal; **Carbohydrates:** 0.74 oz (21.10 g), **Proteins:** 0.43 oz (12.15 g), **Fats:** 0.32 oz (9.08 g); **Fibers:** 0.16 oz (4.40 g).

MICRONUTRIENTS: CALCIUM, POTASSIUM, MAGNESIUM (NATURALLY PRESENT IN GREEK YOGURT, NUTS, CHIA SEEDS, AND FRUIT)

INSTRUCTIONS:

1. **Start with Yogurt:** Grab a bowl and fill it with some creamy low-fat Greek yogurt.
2. **Chia Time:** Sprinkle chia seeds on top of the yogurt and wait a moment to let them settle.
3. **Fruit Layer:** Scatter blueberries and slices of banana across the yogurt.
4. **Nutty Addition:** Toss some chopped nuts over the fruit for a bit of crunch.
5. **Sweet Touch:** Give everything a nice honey drizzle for sweetness.
6. **Mix It Up (Optional):** Give it a gentle stir to mix all those delicious flavors together, if you like.

58. Oat and Dark Chocolate Bars with Hazelnuts

INGREDIENTS: QUANTITY FOR 1 PERSON

- **Oats:** 0.71 oz, about ¼ cup (20g)
- **Dark Chocolate (70% cocoa):** 1.06 oz, about ¼ cup (30g)
- **Low GI Honey:** 0.74 oz, about 1 tablespoon (21g)
- **Chopped Hazelnuts:** 0.35 oz, about 1 tablespoon (10g)

PREPARATION TIME:

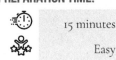

15 minutes

Easy

NUTRITIONAL VALUES (ESTIMATE):

Calories: 235 kcal; **Carbohydrates (CF):** 0.95 oz (27.1g); **Sugars (CA):** 0.32 oz (9.2g); **Fats (F):** 0.46 oz (13.1g); **Proteins (P):** 0.19 oz (5.3g); **Sodium (S):** less than 0.01 oz (1mg)

MICRONUTRIENTS: FIBER, VITAMIN E, PROTEINS

INSTRUCTIONS:

1. **Kick Things Off:** Find a cozy bowl and mix in your oats, chunks of dark chocolate, a hearty splash of honey, and those hazelnuts you've chopped up into tiny treasures. Mix it all up until it feels like they're meant to be together.
2. **Press and Set:** Take that lovely mixture and spread it out in a square baking dish you've lined with parchment paper. Give it a good press with your hands to make sure it's all snug and compact.
3. **Fridge Time:** Now, let the dish take a little chill break in the fridge. Leave it there for a couple of hours to let everything set and become one.
4. **Add a Chocolate Drizzle:** Just before it's done chilling, go ahead and melt some more chocolate. When you pull the dish out of the fridge, drizzle that melted chocolate over the top for an indulgent touch.
5. **Enjoy Your Creation:** Once it's all firm and ready, cut it into snackable bars. There you have it—your very own, perfectly sweet and crunchy treat, ready to make your snack time or dessert moment extra special.

59. Avocado Mash with Sesame Seeds on Whole Grain Crackers

INGREDIENTS: QUANTITY FOR 1 PERSON
- **Mashed Avocado:** 3.53 oz, about ½ avocado (100g)
- **Whole Grain Crackers:** 4 crackers
- **Lemon juice:** 0.53 oz, about 1 tablespoon (15g)
- **Sesame Seeds:** 0.11 oz, about 1 teaspoon (3g)

PREPARATION TIME:

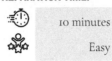 10 minutes

Easy

NUTRITIONAL VALUES (PER SERVING):

Calories: 180 kcal; **Carbohydrates (CF):** 0.39 oz (11g); **Sugars (CA):** 0.35 oz (10g); **Fats (F):** 0.49 oz (14g); **Proteins (P):** 0.11 oz (3g); **Sodium (S):** 0.003 oz (90mg)

MICRONUTRIENTS: FIBER, VITAMIN C, VITAMIN E, POTASSIUM

INSTRUCTIONS:

1. **Avocado Magic:** In a cozy bowl, mash up about half an avocado (100g) until it's perfectly creamy. Add a good squeeze of lemon juice (around a tablespoon or 15g) to brighten it up.
2. **Cracker Layering:** Spread the avocado goodness evenly on four whole grain crackers, making sure every corner gets some love.
3. **Sesame Touch:** Sprinkle a teaspoon (or 3g) of sesame seeds over the top for that extra crunch and a dash of flavor.
4. **Serve It Up:** Dish these out right away for a deliciously quick and healthy treat, perfect for a little snack break or as a simple appetizer.

60. Cinnamon Apple Chips with Dried Fruit and Seeds

INGREDIENTS: QUANTITY FOR 1 PERSON
- **Apple:** 0.46 oz, about 2 tablespoons (13g)
- **Cinnamon:** less than 0.01 oz, about 1/8 teaspoon (0.02g)
- **Chopped Nuts:** 0.18 oz, about 1 teaspoon (5g)
- **Sliced Almonds:** 0.11 oz, about 1/2 teaspoon (3g)
- **Chia Seeds:** 0.04 oz, about 1/4 teaspoon (1g)
- **Coconut Flakes:** 0.04 oz, about 1/2 teaspoon (1g)

PREPARATION TIME:

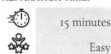 15 minutes

Easy

NUTRITIONAL VALUES (ESTIMATE) (PER SERVING):

Calories: 130 kcal; **Carbohydrates (CF):** 0.5 oz (14g); **Sugars (CA):** 0.28 oz (8g); **Fats (F):** 0.28 oz (8g); **Proteins (P):** 0.07 oz (2g); **Sodium (S):** 0 oz (0mg)

MICRONUTRIENTS: FIBER, VITAMIN E, OMEGA-3

INSTRUCTIONS:

1. **Apple Art:** Start by thinly slicing an apple; think of it as preparation for a delicious art project.
2. **A Cinnamon Whisper:** Dust those apple canvases with just enough cinnamon to give them a hug of sweetness and spice.
3. **Nut Confetti:** Scatter a joyful mix of chopped nuts and almond shards over the slices, bringing a delightful crunch to the mix.
4. **Seeds of Surprise:** Gently sprinkle chia seeds over everything, adding a tiny burst of texture and a dose of health.
5. **Oven Adventure:** Lay your apple slices out on a tray lined with baking paper and let them bake gently until they transform into crispy wonders. Let them take a little rest outside the oven to hit that perfect crunch level.
6. **Taste Test: Now, the best part:** sampling your creation. Grab a crispy slice and let it crunch away in your mouth, savoring the blend of sweetness, spice, and everything nice.

61. Oat and Flaxseed Bars

INGREDIENTS: QUANTITY FOR 1 PERSON

- **Oat flake:** 0.35 oz, about 1/3 cup (10g)
- **Flax Seeds:** 0.11 oz, about 1 teaspoon (3g)
- **Chopped Almonds:** 0.11 oz, about 1/2 teaspoon (3g)
- **Raisins:** 0.11 oz, about 1/2 teaspoon (3g)
- **Honey:** 0.07 oz, about 1/2 teaspoon (2g)
- **Coconut Flakes:** 0.07 oz, about 1/2 teaspoon (2g)
- **Mashed Banana:** 0.11 oz, about 1/2 teaspoon (3g)
- **Cinnamon:** A pinch, less than 1/8 teaspoon (0.02g)

PREPARATION TIME:

15 minutes
Easy

NUTRITIONAL VALUES (ESTIMATE PER SERVING):

Calories: 180 kcal; **Carbohydrates (CF):** 0.73 oz (24g); **Sugars (CA):** 0.46 oz (13g); **Fats (F):** 0.28 oz (8g); **Proteins (P):** 0.11 oz (3g); **Sodium (S):** negligible

MICRONUTRIENTS: FIBER, VITAMIN E, OMEGA-3

INSTRUCTIONS:

1. **Apple Prep Time:** Begin by cutting your apple into super thin slices, getting them ready for snacking greatness.
2. **Sweet Sprinkles:** Dust those thin slices with a bit of cinnamon to add a warm, sweet flair.
3. **Crunchy Toppings:** Sprinkle a fun mix of nuts and almond pieces over your apple slices for that extra crunch.
4. **Seedy Goodness:** Add a little sprinkle of chia seeds for some crunch and a nutritional kick.
5. **Baking Magic:** Place your apple slices on a tray with baking paper and let them bake slowly until they reach the perfect level of crispiness. Give them a moment to cool down for that ultimate crunch.
6. **Snack Time: Now, the best part:** dig in and enjoy the crispy, flavorful snack you've just made.

62. Date and Almond Balls

INGREDIENTS: QUANTITY FOR 1 PERSON

- **Dates:** 0.35 oz, about 1/3 cup (10g)
- **Almonds:** 0.11 oz, about 1/2 teaspoon (3g)
- **Grated Coconut:** 0.07 oz, about 1/2 teaspoon (2g)
- **Chia Seeds:** 0.07 oz, about 1/2 teaspoon (2g)
- **Dried Apple:** 0.11 oz, about 1/2 teaspoon (3g)
- **Raisins:** 0.07 oz, less than 1/2 teaspoon (2g)
- **Coconut Flakes:** 0.04 oz, about 1/4 teaspoon (1g)
- **Cinnamon:** A pinch, less than 1/8 teaspoon (0.02g)

PREPARATION TIME:

15 minutes
Easy

NUTRITIONAL VALUES (ESTIMATE):

Calories: 80 kcal; **Carbohydrates (CF):** 0.56 oz (16g); **Sugars (CA):** 0.39 oz (11g); **Fats (F):** 0.07 oz (2g); **Proteins (P):** 0.04 oz (1g); **Sodium (S):** negligible

MICRONUTRIENTS: FIBER, VITAMIN C, VITAMIN K

INSTRUCTIONS:

1. **Getting the Apples Ready:** First up, slice your apple into ultra-thin pieces, preparing them for a delicious treat.
2. **A Dash of Cinnamon:** Give those slices a gentle shake of cinnamon for a little warmth and sweetness.
3. **Adding Crunch:** Scatter over a playful mix of nuts and almonds, adding a satisfying bite to each slice.
4. **Sprinkle of Seeds:** Toss a few chia seeds on top for an extra bit of texture and a health boost.
5. **Time to Bake:** Spread the slices on a baking sheet lined with parchment and let them bake at a gentle heat until they're just the right kind of crispy. Let them cool to crisp up even more.
6. **Enjoy Your Creation:** Finally, it's time to enjoy the fruits of your labor. Grab a slice, let it crunch in your mouth, and savor the mix of sweet, spicy, and crunchy.

63. Pineapple and Mint Salad

INGREDIENTS: QUANTITY FOR 1 PERSON

- **Pineapple:** 0.46 oz, about 1 tablespoon (13g)
- **Fresh mint leaves:** to taste
- **Chopped Nuts:** 0.14 oz, about 1 teaspoon (4g)
- **Chia Seeds:** 0.07 oz, about 1/2 teaspoon (2g)
- **Sliced Almonds:** 0.11 oz, about 1/2 teaspoon (3g)
- **Sliced Strawberries:** 0.14 oz, about 1 tablespoon (4g)
- **Grated Coconut:** 0.07 oz, about 1/2 teaspoon (2g)
- **Dark Chocolate Flakes:** 0.04 oz, about 1/4 teaspoon (1g)

PREPARATION TIME:

15 minutes

Easy

NUTRITIONAL VALUES (ESTIMATE):

Calories: 85 kcal; **Total Carbohydrates:** 8.14 oz (231g); **Fats:** 4.48 oz (127g); **Proteins:** 2.32 oz (66g); **Sodium:** 0.01 oz (0.28g).

INSTRUCTIONS:

1. **Getting the Apples Ready:** First up, slice your apple into ultra-thin pieces, preparing them for a delicious treat.
2. **A Dash of Cinnamon:** Give those slices a gentle shake of cinnamon for a little warmth and sweetness.
3. **Adding Crunch:** Scatter over a playful mix of nuts and almonds, adding a satisfying bite to each slice.
4. **Sprinkle of Seeds:** Toss a few chia seeds on top for an extra bit of texture and a health boost.
5. **Time to Bake:** Spread the slices on a baking sheet lined with parchment and let them bake at a gentle heat until they're just the right kind of crispy. Let them cool to crisp up even more.
6. **Enjoy Your Creation:** Finally, it's time to enjoy the fruits of your labor. Grab a slice, let it crunch in your mouth, and savor the mix of sweet, spicy, and crunchy.

64. Ricotta Cup with Honey and Nuts

INGREDIENTS: QUANTITY FOR 1 PERSON.

- **Ricotta:** 1.41 oz, about 3 tablespoons (40g)
- **Honey:** 0.04 oz, less than 1/4 teaspoon (1g)
- **Chopped Nuts:** 0.07 oz, about 1/2 teaspoon (2g)
- **Sliced Strawberries:** 0.18 oz, about 1 tablespoon (5g)
- **Sliced Almonds:** 0.11 oz, about 1/2 teaspoon (3g).
- **Chia Seeds:** 0.07 oz, about 1/2 teaspoon (2g)
- **Grated Coconut:** 0.07 oz, about 1/2 teaspoon (2g)
- **Dark Chocolate Flakes:** 0.04 oz, about 1/4 teaspoon (1g)

PREPARATION TIME:

10 minutes.

Easy

NUTRITIONAL VALUES (ESTIMATE):

Calories: 159 kcal; **Total Carbohydrates:** 4.27 oz (121g); **Fats:** 8.65 oz (245g); **Proteins:** 9.09 oz (258g); **Sodium:** 0.23 oz (6.5g).

INSTRUCTIONS:

1. **Filling the Cup:** Grab your coziest cup or bowl and fill it with smooth ricotta as the base.
2. **Sweet Honey:** Pour a sweet stream of honey over the ricotta to sweeten it up..
3. **Crunchy Nuts:** Toss in some chopped nuts for a crunchy contrast to the creamy ricotta.
4. **Strawberries on Top:** Add a layer of vibrant, sliced strawberries for a fresh, fruity twist.
5. **Almonds and Chia:** Dust the top with sliced almonds and a sprinkle of chia seeds for a bit of crunch and a health kick.
6. **Final Touches:** Garnish with a sprinkle of grated coconut and a few dark chocolate flakes for a luxurious finish.
7. **Time to Dig In:** Your ricotta cup is now a masterpiece ready to be savored, blending rich flavors and varied textures into a perfect snack or dessert treat..

65. Dried Fruit and Seed Mix

INGREDIENTS: QUANTITY FOR 1 PERSON

- **Almonds:** 0.04 oz, less than 1/4 teaspoon (1g)
- **Walnuts:** 0.04 oz, less than 1/4 teaspoon (1g).
- **Sunflower Seeds:** 0.04 oz, less than 1/4 teaspoon (1g)
- **Raisins:** 0.11 oz, about 1/2 teaspoon (3g)
- **Dried Apple:** 0.11 oz, about 1/2 teaspoon (3g)
- **Chia Seeds:** 0.07 oz, about 1/2 teaspoon (2g)
- **Grated Coconut:** 0.07 oz, about 1/2 teaspoon (2g).
- **Dark Chocolate Flakes:** 0.07 oz, about 1/2 teaspoon (2g)

PREPARATION TIME:

15 minutes

Easy

NUTRITIONAL VALUES (ESTIMATE):.

Calories: 56 kcal; **Total Carbohydrates:** 6.57 oz (186g); **Fats:** 3.21 oz (91g); **Proteins:** 1.46 oz (41g); **Sodium:** 0.02 oz (0.5g).

INSTRUCTIONS:

1. **Creating the Mix:** Grab a bowl and throw in a bunch of goodies—almonds, walnuts, sunflower seeds, raisins, bits of dried apple, chia seeds, some grated coconut, and dark chocolate flakes. Give it all a good stir to mix it up.
2. **Snack Time:** Now it's ready to be your go-to healthy snack or a quick munch. Dive into the tasty blend of flavors and savor the nutritional goodness each bite offers

66. Banana and Coconut Ice Cream.

INGREDIENTS: QUANTITY FOR 1 PERSON

- **Banana:** 0.35 oz, about 1 tablespoon mashed (10g)
- **Coconut Milk:** 0.11 oz, less than 1 teaspoon (3g)
- **Honey:** 0.07 oz, less than 1/2 teaspoon (2g)
- **Chopped Nuts:** 0.11 oz, about 1/2 teaspoon (3g).
- **Ground Flax Seeds:** 0.07 oz, less than 1/2 teaspoon (2g)
- **Coconut Flakes:** 0.07 oz, less than 1/2 teaspoon (2g)
- **Dried Cherries:** 0.11 oz, about 1/2 teaspoon (3g)

PREPARATION TIME:

13 minutes.

Medium

NUTRITIONAL VALUES (ESTIMATE):

Calories: 106 kcal; **Total Carbohydrates:** 16.54 oz (469g); **Fats:** 3.64 oz (103g); **Proteins:** 1.86 oz (53g); **Sodium:** 0.02 oz (0.6g)

INSTRUCTIONS:

1. **Making the base:** Grab a banana and give it a good mash in your bowl until it's nice and creamy. Add a splash of coconut milk and a hint of honey for a sweet touch.
2. **Mixing in Fun Stuff:** Throw in a bunch of nuts, a sprinkle of flaxseeds, coconut flakes, and dried cherries. Stir it up well so every bite's got a bit of everything.
3. **Freezing:** Pour the mixture into a container and let it freeze until it's solid, roughly a couple of hours.
4. **Before Enjoying:** Let the ice cream sit out for a bit to soften up, making it just right for scooping.
5. **Garnish and Dig In:** Add a little extra something on top for flair, then enjoy your homemade banana and coconut ice cream masterpiece. It's a small batch of happiness, made by you.

67. Pears with Blue Cheese.

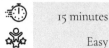

INGREDIENTS: QUANTITY FOR 1 SERVING

- **Pear (CF):** 0.35 oz (about 1/4 of a small pear)
- **Blue Cheese (F, P):** 0.11 oz (less than 1 teaspoon)
- **Chopped Almonds (F, P):** 0.14 oz (about 1 teaspoon)
- **Honey (CF):** 0.07 oz (less than 1/2 teaspoon).
- **Pumpkin Seeds (F, P):** 0.11 oz (about 1/2 teaspoon)
- **Dried Figs (CF):** 0.14 oz (about 1 small fig)
- **Coconut Flakes (F):** 0.07 oz (about 1/2 teaspoon)
- **Cinnamon (CF):** A pinch (about 1/8 teaspoon)

PREPARATION TIME:.

15 minutes

Easy

NUTRITIONAL VALUES (ESTIMATE FOR 1 SERVING):

Calories: 80 kcal; **Carbohydrates:** 10g; **Proteins:** 1g; **Fats:** 4g; **Fiber:** 2g.

INSTRUCTIONS:

1. **Prepare the ingredients:** Slice a small pear into thin slices. Crumble the blue cheese finely. Chop the almonds to get about 1 teaspoon. Cut a small, dried fig into pieces..
2. **Assemble the appetizer:** Arrange the pear slices on a plate. Evenly distribute the crumbled blue cheese over the pear slices. Add the chopped almonds and the cut dried figs.
3. Add honey and pumpkin seeds. Drizzle honey gently over the pears and cheese. Add pumpkin seeds for a touch of crunchiness.
4. **Sprinkle Coconut Flakes and Cinnamon:** Finish the appetizer by distributing coconut flakes over the preparation. Add a pinch of cinnamon for a touch of warmth and aroma.
5. **Serve:** Your pears with blue cheese are ready to be enjoyed as an appetizer. Savor slowly and appreciate the combination of sweet and savory flavors. Bon appétit!

68. Mini Spelt and Banana Pancakes

INGREDIENTS: QUANTITY FOR 1 PERSON

- **Spelt Flour (CF):** 0.35 oz (about 10g, about 2/3 tablespoon)
- **Banana (CF):** 0.11 oz (about 3g, about 1/4 of a small banana).
- **Egg (P):** 1/8 of an egg (about 0.35 oz)
- **Chopped Almonds (F, P):** 0.14 oz (about 4g, about 1 teaspoon)
- **Honey (CF):** 0.07 oz (about 2g, less than 1/2 teaspoon)
- **Ground Flax Seeds (CF, F, P):** 0.11 oz (about 3g, about 1/2 teaspoon)
- **Almond Milk (F):** 0.35 oz (about 10ml, about 2 teaspoons).
- **Coconut Flakes (F):** 0.04 oz (about 1g, about 1/4 teaspoon)
- **Cinnamon (CF):** A pinch (about 0.02g, about 1/8 teaspoon)

COOKING TIME:

15 minutes

10 minutes.

5 minutes

Easy

NUTRITIONAL VALUES (FOR 1 PERSON):

Calories: 150 kcal; **Total Carbohydrates:** 21 oz (about 595g); **Proteins:** 4 oz (about 113g); **Fats:** 6 oz (about 170g); **Fiber:** 0.11 oz (about 3g)

INSTRUCTIONS:

1. **Whip Up the Base:** Start by mashing a banana until it's completely smooth. Stir in a bit of coconut milk and a drizzle of honey for that perfect sweetness..
2. **Toss in the Goodies:** Add a mix of crunchy nuts, a bit of flaxseed for health, some coconut flakes for flavor, and dried cherries for a sweet surprise. Give it all a good stir.
3. **Freeze It:** Scoop your mix into a container and pop it into the freezer. Wait for about 2-3 hours, or until it's all firmed up.
4. **Soften for Scooping:** Let your ice cream warm up just a tad outside the freezer, making it easier to scoop.
5. **Final Touches:** Sprinkle a little extra on top for decoration, then dive into your very own delicious banana and coconut ice cream treat. It's your little creation, ready to make your day brighter.

69. Seed Crackers and Chickpea Hummus

INGREDIENTS: QUANTITY FOR 1 PERSON

- **Flax Seeds:** 0.35 oz, about 2 teaspoons (10g); Chia Seeds: 0.35 oz, about 2 teaspoons (10g); Almond flour: 0.7 oz, about 2 tablespoons (20g).
- **Water:** 1.05 oz, about 2 tablespoons (30ml); Cooked Chickpeas: 1.76 oz, about 1/4 cup (50g); Tahini (sesame paste): 0.35 oz, about 2 teaspoons (10g); Extra Virgin Olive Oil: 0.18 oz, about 1 teaspoon (5g); Lemon (juice): 0.35 oz, about 2 teaspoons (10ml).
- **Carrots:** 1.41 oz, about 1/4 cup cut into sticks (40g)

COOKING TIME:

30 minutes

20 minutes

10 minutes.

Easy

NUTRITIONAL VALUES (ESTIMATE):

Kcal: ~150 kcal; **CF (Carbohydrates with Fiber):** 0.88 oz (25g); **CA (Starchy Carbohydrates):** 0.44 oz (12.5g); **F (Fats):** 0.35 oz (10g); **P (Proteins):** 0.35 oz (10g); **S (Sodium):** Varies depending on added salt.

MICRONUTRIENTS: VITAMIN A, VITAMIN C, POTASSIUM, FIBER

INSTRUCTIONS:

1. **Savory Cracker:** Begin by mixing flax seeds, chia seeds, almond flour, and water in a bowl until you achieve a homogeneous mixture. Take a baking sheet, line it with parchment paper, and spread the mixture onto it.
2. **Bake it:** at 180°C (356°F) for about 8-10 minutes, checking the color during cooking to ensure it is nicely golden but not too dark.
3. **Hummus Creation:** Place cooked chickpeas, tahini, a bit of olive oil, and a splash of lemon juice in a blender. Blend everything until you get a super smooth and inviting consistency.
4. **Carrot Sticks Prep:** Give the carrots a quick wash and chop them into stick shapes for easy dipping.
5. **Time to Serve:** Lay out your freshly baked seed crackers on a plate, scoop up some of that creamy hummus, and arrange the carrot sticks for a crunchy contrast. Dive into this tasty, wholesome snack whenever you need a little pick-me-up.

70. Mini Chickpea, Vegetable, and Light Basil Pesto Salad

INGREDIENTS: QUANTITY FOR 1 PERSON

- **Chickpeas:** 3.17 oz, about ½ cup (90g)
- **Cherry Tomatoes:** 2.65 oz, about ½ cup (75g)
- **Cucumber:** 1.41 oz, about ¼ cup (40g)
- **Light Basil Pesto:** 1.06 oz, about 2 tablespoons (30g)
- **Preparation time:**
- **Total:** 10 minutes
- **Preparation:** 10 minutes

0 minutes

Very easy

NUTRITIONAL VALUES (ESTIMATE):

Calories: 237.4 kcal; **Carbohydrates:** 30.27 g; **Proteins:** 9.76 g; **Fats:** 9.69 g; **Fibers:** 8.42 g; **Sodium:** 129.35 mg.

MICRONUTRIENTS: IRON, MAGNESIUM, POTASSIUM (NATURALLY PRESENT IN CHICKPEAS, TOMATOES, CUCUMBER, AND BASIL)

INSTRUCTIONS:

1. **Getting the Chickpeas Ready:** Start with the chickpeas – give them a quick rinse and drain if you grabbed them from a can. Or, for an extra touch of freshness, go for chickpeas you've soaked and cooked up yourself.
2. **Chopping the veggies:** Give those cherry tomatoes a wash and slice them in half. Then, peel the cucumber and chop it into bite-sized pieces or thin slices, just how you like it.
3. **Mixing it All Together:** In a mixing bowl, bring together the chickpeas, halved cherry tomatoes, chopped cucumber, and a splash of light basil pesto. Mix it all gently, so every bit gets a kiss of pesto.
4. **Serving Time:** Scoop your salad into a nice bowl or plate. It's yummy right away, but if you have time, let it chill in the fridge for a little while to let those flavors really come together.

8.5. Desserts and Cakes
(Even though they are sweets and cakes for diabetics, don't overdo it!)

71. Apple Pie

INGREDIENTS: QUANTITY FOR 4 PEOPLE

- **Low glycemic index apples:** 17 oz, about 4 medium apples (480g)
- **Erythritol or stevia:** 4.23 oz, about 1/2 cup (120g)
- **Ground cinnamon:** 1 teaspoon
- **Nutmeg:** 1/4 teaspoon
- **Whole wheat flour or almond flour for the crust:** 4.23 oz, about 1 cup (120g)
- **Unsalted butter or trans-fat-free margarine:** 3.95 oz, about 1/2 cup (112g)

COOKING TIME:

	45 minutes
	15 minutes
	30 minutes
	Easy

NUTRITIONAL VALUES (PER SERVING):

Calories: 230; **Carbohydrates (CF):** 12g / 0.42 oz; **Sugars (CA):** 40g / 1.41 oz; **Fats (F):** 8g / 0.28 oz; **Proteins (P):** 2g / 0.07 oz. **Sodium (S):** 160mg.

MICRONUTRIENTS: FIBER, VITAMIN C, CALCIUM, POTASSIUM

PREPARATION:

1. **Heat the oven in advance:** Set the oven to 180°C (350°F).
2. **Peel, slice, and cut:** the apples into thin slices.
3. **In a large bowl, mix:** the apples with the sweetener, cinnamon, and nutmeg.
4. **In another bowl, prepare the crust:** by mixing the whole wheat or almond flour with the butter or margarine until sandy in texture.
5. **Line a pie dish:** with half of the crust.
6. **Apple Mixture:** Pour the apple mixture onto the crust.
7. **Cover with the remaining crust:** in strips or lattice.
8. **Bake in the oven:** for about 30 minutes, or until the crust is golden and the apples are tender.
9. **Serve hot:** or at room temperature; it's good either way.

72. Cheesecake

INGREDIENTI: QUANTITY FOR 4 PEOPLE

- **Reduced-fat cream cheese:** 16.93 oz, about 2 cups (480g)
- **Low glycemic index sweetener:** 8.47 oz, about 1 cup (240g)
- **Vanilla extract:** 0.18 oz, about 1 teaspoon (5g)
- **Eggs:** 3.53 oz, about 2 medium eggs (100g)
- **Almond flour or low-carb biscuits for the crust:** 4.23 oz, about 1 cup (120g)
- **Fresh fruit or sugar-free fruit sauce for garnish (as desired)**

COOKING TIME:

 1 hour and 20 minutes

 20 minutes

1 hour

Medium

NUTRITIONAL VALUES (PER SERVING):

Calories: approximately 320; **Carbohydrates (CF):** 0.63 oz (about 18g); **Sugars (CA):** 0.49 oz (about 14g); **Fats (F):** 0.78 oz (about 22g); **Proteins (P):** 0.35 oz (about 10g); **Sodium (S):** 0.01 oz (about 280mg).

MICRONUTRIENTS: CALCIUM, PROTEINS, VITAMIN D

PREPARATION:

1. **Warming Up:** Kick things off by getting your oven hot and ready at 160°C (325°F).
2. **Mixing the Good Stuff:** Grab your cream cheese, sweetener, and a dash of vanilla and mix them up until they're super smooth. Then, crack the eggs in one by one, giving each a good stir.
3. **Crust Creation:** Take your almond flour or crumbled biscuits and press them down into the bottom of an 8-inch springform pan to make a nice, firm base.
4. **Filling It Up:** Carefully pour your creamy mixture over the prepared crust and let it bake for about an hour, or until it looks just right and is set.
5. **Cooling Down:** Once it's done, turn off the oven, but leave your cheesecake inside to chill for another hour. After that, pop it in the fridge to get really cold for at least 4 hours, or even better, overnight.
6. **Final Touches:** Just before you're ready to serve, jazz it up with some fresh fruit or a drizzle of sugar-free fruit sauce to make it look as good as it tastes.

73. Brownies

INGREDIENTS: QUANTITY FOR 4 PEOPLE

- **Unsweetened cocoa powder:** 2.12 oz, about 1/2 cup (60g)
- **Almond flour or coconut flour:** 2.12 oz, about 1/2 cup (60g)
- **Low glycemic index sweetener:** 8.47 oz, about 1 cup (240g)
- **Unsalted butter or coconut oil:** 3.95 oz, about 1/2 cup (112g)
- **Eggs:** 3.53 oz, about 2 medium eggs (100g)
- **Vanilla extract:** 1 teaspoon
- **Chopped nuts (optional):** 2.12 oz, about 1/2 cup (60g)

COOKING TIME:

	30 minutes
	15 minutes
	15 minutes
	Easy

NUTRITIONAL VALUES (PER SERVING):

Calories: 280; Carbohydrates (CF): 21g; Sugars (CA): 30g; Fats (F): 18g; Proteins (P): 6g; Sodium (S): 140mg.

MICRONUTRIENTS: MAGNESIUM, POTASSIUM, PROTEINS

PREPARATION:

1. **Heat the oven in advance:** Set the oven to 180°C (350°F).
2. **Almonds, Coconut, & Cocoa:** Take a bowl and mix the cocoa powder, almond flour, or coconut flour, and the sweetener.
3. **Melt everything:** Take a saucepan and melt the butter or coconut oil.
4. **Turn off the heat:** Remove it from the heat and add the vanilla extract.
5. **Let's mix!** Pour the melted butter or coconut oil into the bowl with the ingredients and mix.
6. **Now add the eggs:** and mix until a homogeneous mixture is obtained. If desired, add the chopped nuts and mix.
7. **Into the oven:** Pour the batter into a square or rectangular baking pan lined with parchment paper.
8. **Oven time:** Bake for about 15 minutes or until the edges are set but the center is still slightly soft.
9. **Let it cool:** Turn it off and let it cool, then cut it into squares.

74. Pecan Pie

INGREDIENTS: QUANTITY FOR 4 PEOPLE

- **Pecan nuts:** 4.23 oz (about 120g)
- **Low glycemic index sweetener (light agave syrup or sugar-free maple syrup):** 8.47 oz (about 240ml)
- **Egg:** 7.05 oz (about 2 medium eggs, 200g)
- **Unsalted butter:** 2 oz (about 4 tablespoons, 56g)
- **Vanilla extract:** 0.18 oz (about 1 teaspoon, 5g)
- **Whole wheat flour or almond flour for the crust:** 4.23 oz (about 120g)

COOKING TIME:

	60 minutes
	15 minutes
	45 minutes
	Medium

NUTRITIONAL VALUES (ESTIMATED):

Calories: environ 320 g; Carbohydrates (CF): 0.92 oz (about 26g); Sugars (CA): 0.28 oz (about 8g); Fats (F): 0.78 oz (about 22g); Proteins (P): 0.18 oz (about 5g); Sodium (S): 0.005 oz (about 160mg)

INSTRUCTIONS:

1. **Preheat:** the oven to 175°C (350°F).
2. **Prepare the crust:** In a bowl, combine the flour with 2 tablespoons of butter and a little water, mixing until you get a malleable dough. Roll out the dough in a pie dish and set it aside.
3. **Make the filling:** In another bowl, combine the eggs, sweetener, melted butter (remaining 2 tablespoons), and vanilla extract until you get a homogeneous mixture..
4. **Assemble the pie:** Arrange the pecan nuts on the prepared crust.
5. Pour the filling over the pecan nuts in the pie dish.
6. **Bake:** Place the pie in the oven and bake for about 45 minutes, or until it becomes golden and the filling is set.
7. **Cooling:** Allow the pecan pie to cool before serving, allowing the filling to further solidify.

75. Banana Split

INGREDIENTS: QUANTITY FOR 4 PEOPLE:

- **Bananas:** 4 (16 oz, about 480g)
- **Sugar-free ice cream (vanilla, chocolate, and strawberry):** 2 cups (16 oz, about 480ml)
- **Sugar-free chocolate syrup:** 1/4 cup (2 oz, about 60ml).
- **Sugar-free whipped cream:** 1 cup (8 oz, about 240ml)
- **Chopped nuts:** 1/4 cup (1 oz, about 30g)
- **Sugar-free cherries for garnish:** 4 cherries

NUTRITIONAL VALUES (ESTIMATED PER SERVING):

Calories: 180 kcal; **Total Carbohydrates:** 20g (about 568g); **Fats:** 10g (about 284g); **Proteins:** 2g (about 57g); **Sodium:** 50mg (about 0.00176 oz).

MICRONUTRIENTS: POTASSIUM, MAGNESIUM, CALCIUM, PROTEINS

INSTRUCTIONS:

1. **Preparing the Bananas:** Peel the bananas and cut them in half lengthwise. Then, arrange two banana halves on each plate.
2. **Adding the Ice Cream:** Scoop sugar-free vanilla, chocolate, and strawberry ice cream over the bananas, offering a variety of flavors.
3. **Pouring the Chocolate Syrup:** Drizzle 2 oz of sugar-free chocolate syrup over each serving to enhance the taste.
4. **Garnishing:** Add 2 oz of sugar-free whipped cream on each banana split, sprinkle with 1 oz of chopped nuts, and top with a sugar-free cherry.
5. **Immediate Service:** Serve immediately to enjoy the combination of flavors and textures at its best.

76. Tiramisù

INGREDIENTS: FOR 4 PEOPLE

- **Ladyfingers (sugar-free or homemade with almond flour and low-glycemic sweetener):** 12, approximately 5.29 oz (150g)
- **Mascarpone:** 8.47 oz, 1 cup (240g)
- **Eggs:** 3, approximately 5.29 oz (150g)
- **Low-glycemic sweetener (erythritol or stevia):** 4.23 oz, ½ cup (120g)
- **Unsweetened coffee:** 8.47 oz, 1 cup (240ml)
- **Unsweetened cocoa powder:** for garnish

COOKING TIME:

240 minutes (needs to rest in the fridge)

30 minutes

None

Medium

NUTRITIONAL VALUES (ESTIMATE PER SERVING):

Calories: 280 kcal; **Total Carbohydrates:** 0.85 oz (24g); **Sugars:** 0.28 oz (8g); **Fats:** 0.71 oz (20g); **Proteins:** 0.25 oz (7g); **Sodium:** 0.0049 oz (140mg).

MICRONUTRIENTS: POTASSIUM, CALCIUM, IRON, PROTEIN

DIRECTIONS:

1. Prepare the coffee and let it cool.
2. Mix the mascarpone with the sweetener in a bowl until smooth.
3. Separate the eggs. In another bowl, beat the yolks and then incorporate them into the mascarpone mixture.
4. **Beat the egg whites:** until stiff peaks form, then gently fold them into the Mascarpone mixture to keep the texture light and airy.
5. Dip the ladyfingers quickly in coffee to avoid soaking them too much, then create a first layer in a dish.
6. Cover with half of the mascarpone mixture, spreading evenly.
7. Add another layer of coffee-dipped ladyfingers, and top with the remaining mascarpone mixture.
8. Refrigerate for at least 4 hours, or preferably overnight, to allow the flavors to meld and the dessert to firm up.
9. Before serving, sprinkle with unsweetened cocoa powder for a classic finish.

77. Low-Carb Baklava

INGREDIENTS: QUANTITY FOR 4 PEOPLE:

- **Whole wheat or low-carb phyllo pastry sheets:** 12 sheets (about 16.93 oz, 480g)
- **Chopped nuts (almonds, walnuts, pistachios):** 4.23 oz, about 1 cup (120g)
- **Unsalted butter:** 4.06 oz, about 1/2 cup (115g)
- **Low-glycemic index sweetener (light agave syrup or artificial honey):** 8.47 oz, about 1 cup (240ml)
- **Cinnamon:** 0.07 oz, about 1 teaspoon (2g)

COOKING TIME:

⏱	45 minutes
🍲	15 minutes
👨‍🍳	30 minutes
❀	Medium

NUTRITIONAL VALUES (ESTIMATED PER SERVING):

Calories: 350 kcal; **Total Carbohydrates:** 0.85 oz (about 24g); **Added Sugars:** 0.99 oz (about 28g); **Fats:** 0.81 oz (about 23g); **Proteins:** 0.25 oz (about 7g); **Sodium:** 0.006 oz (about 170mg).

MICRONUTRIENTS: CALCIUM, MAGNESIUM, VITAMIN E

INSTRUCTIONS:

1. **Phyllo Pastry Preparation:** Begin by brushing a sheet of phyllo pastry with melted butter, then layer and brush another sheet, continuing this process.
2. **Adding the Nuts:** Spread the chopped nuts over every second sheet of phyllo pastry.
3. **Building the Baklava:** Layer the prepared sheets, alternating between phyllo pastry and nuts, until all materials are used up.
4. **Preparing for Baking:** Cut into squares or diamonds before baking.
5. **Baking:** Bake at 175°C for 30 minutes or until golden brown.
6. **Prepare the syrup:** Mix sweetener, water, and cinnamon, then bring to a boil and let it cool.
7. **Finish the Baklava:** Pour the syrup over the freshly baked, hot baklava.
8. **Cooling:** Allow to cool completely before serving.

78. Crème Brûlée

INGREDIENTS: QUANTITY FOR 4 PEOPLE

- **Heavy cream:** 16 ounces (2 cups, 480ml)
- **Egg yolks:** 6 yolks
- **Low-glycemic index sweetener:** 4.23 ounces (1/2 cup, 120g)
- **Vanilla extract:** 0.18 ounces (1 teaspoon, 5ml)
- **Substitute powdered sugar for caramelizing (optional):** 0.53 ounces (1 tablespoon, 15g)

COOKING TIME:

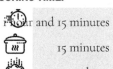
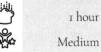

hour and 15 minutes

15 minutes

1 hour

Medium

NUTRITIONAL VALUES (ESTIMATED PER SERVING):

Calories: 330 kcal; **Total carbohydrates:** 1.02 ounces (about 29g); **Added sugars:** 0.74 ounces (about 21g); **Fats:** 0.74 ounces (about 21g); **Proteins:** 0.25 ounces (about 7g); **Sodium:** 0.0014 ounces (about 40mg).

MICRONUTRIENTS: CALCIUM, VITAMIN D, IRON

INSTRUCTIONS:

1. Preheat the oven to 150°C (302°F).
2. Heat the cream over medium heat without bringing it to a boil.
3. Beat the egg yolks with the sweetener and vanilla extract in a bowl.
4. Gradually add the hot cream to the yolks, stirring constantly.
5. Pour the mixture into crème brûlée dishes.
6. Bake in a water bath in the oven for about 1 hour.
7. Cool in the refrigerator for at least 2 hours.
8. Caramelize the substitute powdered sugar on the surface using a kitchen torch before serving.

79. Diabetic Sacher Torte

INGREDIENTS: QUANTITY FOR 4 PEOPLE

- **Almond flour or low-carb flour:** 4.23 oz, about 1 cup (120g)
- **Unsweetened cocoa powder:** 1.76 oz, about 1/2 cup (50g)
- **Low-glycemic index sweetener:** 4.23 oz, about 1/2 cup (120g)
- **Eggs:** 4 eggs (about 7.05 oz, 200g)
- **Unsalted butter:** 4.05 oz, about 1/2 cup (115g)
- **Sugar-free apricot jam:** 4.23 oz, about 1/2 cup (120g)

COOKING TIME:

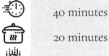

40 minutes

20 minutes

20 minutes

Medium

NUTRITIONAL VALUES (ESTIMATED):

Calories: 330 kcal; **Total Carbohydrates:** 0.81 oz (about 23g); **Added Sugars:** 0.85 oz (about 24g); **Fats:** 0.81 oz (about 23g); **Proteins:** 0.35 oz (about 10g); **Sodium:** 0.0056 oz (about 160mg).

MICRONUTRIENTS: CALCIUM, IRON, VITAMIN E

INSTRUCTIONS:

1. Preheat the oven to 180°C (356°F).
2. **Prepare the batter:** Mix almond flour, cocoa, and sweetener in a bowl.
3. Add the eggs and melted butter, stirring until a homogeneous batter is obtained.
4. Pour the batter into a greased and floured pan.
5. Bake for about 20 minutes or until fully cooked.
6. Let the cake cool, then spread the apricot jam over the surface.

80. Low-Carb Pastel de Nata

INGREDIENTS: QUANTITY FOR 4 PEOPLE

- **Low-carb puff pastry:** 8.11 oz, about 1 package (230g)
- **Egg yolks:** 4.23 oz, about 4 yolks (120g)
- **Low-glycemic index sweetener:** 2.12 oz, about 4 tablespoons (60g)
- **Cream:** 8.45 oz, about 1 cup (240ml)
- **Vanilla extract:** 0.17 oz, about 1 teaspoon (5ml)
- **Cinnamon:** a sprinkle for garnish

COOKING TIME:

 45 minutes

 15 minutes

30 minutes

Medium

NUTRITIONAL VALUES (ESTIMATED PER SERVING):

Calories: 285 kcal; **Total Carbohydrates:** 0.6 oz (about 17g); **Sugars:** 0.42 oz (about 12g); **Fats:** 0.67 oz (about 19g); **Proteins:** 0.21 oz (about 6g); **Sodium:** 0.0037 oz (about 105mg).

MICRONUTRIENTS: CALCIUM, IRON

INSTRUCTIONS:

1. **Dough Preparation:** Beat together egg yolks, sweetener, and vanilla extract until smooth.
2. **Heating the Cream:** Warm the cream without boiling it, then gradually incorporate it into the egg mixture.
3. **Base Preparation:** Roll out the puff pastry into the molds, shaping it to fit the edges.
4. **Baking:** Pour the egg mixture into the puff pastry bases, add a sprinkle of cinnamon, and bake at 220°C for 30 minutes.
5. **Serving:** Allow the Pastel de Nata to cool before serving.

Chapter 9
Meal Plan and Index

9.1 BONUS 1: Meal plan 30 Days

	Day 1	Day 2	Day 3
Breakfast	**6.** Bell Pepper and Light Cheddar Omelette with Whole Wheat Bread	**2.** Oatmeal, Blueberry, and Cinnamon Muffins	**3.** Spinach and Light Feta Frittata
Snack 1	**63.** Pineapple and Mint Salad	**59.** Avocado Mash with Sesame Seeds on Whole Grain Crackers	**56.** Oat and Blueberry Mini Muffins
Lunch	**16.** Mediterranean Chicken Salad with Whole Wheat Bread	**17.** Baked Salmon with Vegetables	**19.** Tofu and Vegetables Stir-Fry with Beneficial Spices
Snack 2	**60.** Cinnamon Apple Chips with Dried Fruit and Seeds	**58.** Oat and Dark Chocolate Bars with Hazelnuts	**64.** Ricotta Cup with Honey and Nuts
Dinner	**40.** Chicken Stuffed with Spinach and Feta	**37.** Grilled Turkey with Steamed Asparagus	**38.** Eggplant and Chickpea Stew

	Day 4	Day 5	Day 6
Breakfast	**4.** Avocado Toast with Poached Egg and Turmeric	**5.** Greek Yogurt with Nuts, Honey, Almonds, and Chia Seeds	**1.** Whole Wheat Pancakes with Sugar-Free Maple Syrup
Snack 1	**65.** Dried Fruit and Seed Mix	**69.** Seed Crackers and Chickpea Hummus	**62.** Date and Almond Balls
Lunch	**28.** Whole Wheat Spaghetti with Tomato and Basil	**29.** Turkey Chili	**31.** Chicken and Vegetable Wrap
Snack 2	**63.** Pineapple and Mint Salad	**68.** Mini Spelt and Banana Pancakes	**64.** Ricotta Cup with Honey and Nuts
Dinner	**39.** Baked Cod with Tomato, Rosemary, and Turmeric	**42.** Turkey and Vegetable Skillet Ingredients: Quantity for 1 person	**46.** Chicken and Mushroom Soup

	Day 7	Day 8	Day 9
Breakfast	7. Quinoa and Cinnamon Porridge with Apples and Bananas	6. Bell Pepper and Light Cheddar Omelette with Whole Wheat Bread	11. Toast with Ricotta and Grilled Peaches
Snack 1	65. Dried Fruit and seed Mix	61. Oat and Flaxseed Bars	62. Date and Almond Balls
Lunch	17. Baked Salmon with Vegetables	18. Lentil Soup	20. Quinoa and Black Bean Salad with Corn and Avocado
Snack 2	68. Mini Salt and Banana Pancakes	67. Pears with Blue Cheese	69. Seed Crackers and Chickpea Hummus
Dinner	51. Lemon and Thyme Chicken With Streamed Vegetables	43. Stir-Fried Beef and Broccoli	45. Grilled Salmon and Avocado Salad

	Day 10	Day 11	Day 12
Breakfast	12. Sweet Potato Waffles with Cinnamon and Turmeric	13. Whole Wheat Crepes with Ricotta and Raspberries	15. Berry and Chia Seed Smoothie Bowl
Snack 1	63. Pineapple and Mint Salad	64. Ricotta Cup with Honey and Nuts	66. Banana and Coconut Ice Cream
Lunch	21. Chicken and Couscous Salad with Grilled Vegetables	19. Tofu and Vegetables Stir-Fry with Beneficial Spices	29. Turkey Chili
Snack 2	70. Mini Chickpea, Vegetable, and Light Basil Pesto Salad	65. Dried Fruit and Seed Mix	60. Cinnamon Apple Chips with Dried Fruit and Seeds
Dinner	46. Chicken and Mushroom Soup	50. Ratatouille with Polenta	53. Minestrone with Barley and Vegetables

	Day 13	Day 14	Day 15
Breakfast	7. Quinoa and Cinnamon Porridge with Apples and Bananas	8. Whole Wheat Waffles with Fresh Fruit	10. Breakfast Burrito with Turkey and Avocado
Snack 1	61. Oat and Flaxseed Bars	56. Oat and Blueberry Mini Muffins	69. Seed Crackers and Chickpea Hummus
Lunch	27. Curry Chicken with Brown Rice and Vegetables	28. Whole Wheat Spaghetti with Tomato and Basil	27. Curry Chicken with Brown Rice and Vegetables
Snack 2	68. Mini Spelt and Banana Pancakes	61. Oat and Flaxseed Bars	67. Pears with Blue Cheese
Dinner	41. Stir-Fried Tofu and Vegetables	51. Lemon and Thyme Chicken with Steamed Vegetables	41. Stir-Fried Tofu and Vegetables

	Day 16	Day 17	Day 18
Breakfast	4. Avocado Toast with Poached Egg and Turmeric	12. Sweet Potato Waffles with Cinnamon and Turmeric	5. Greek Yogurt with Nuts, Almonds, and Chia seeds
Snack 1	62. Date and Almond Balls	64. Ricotta Cup with Honey and Nuts	57. Greek Yogurt with Nuts and Fruit
Lunch	32. Barley Salad with Vegetables and Feta	28. Whole Wheat Spaghetti with Tomato and Basil	29. Turkey Chili
Snack 2	63. Pineapple and Mint Salad	66. Banana and Coconut Ice Cream	68. Mini Spelt and Banana Pancakes
Dinner	43. Stir-Fried Beef and Broccoli	38. Eggplant and Chickpea Stew	55. Chicken and Vegetable Skewers

	Day 19	Day 20	Day 21
Breakfast	8. Whole Wheat Waffles with Fresh Fruit	15. Berry and Chia Seed Smoothie Bowl	8. Whole Wheat Waffles with Fresh Fruit
Snack 1	63. Pineapple and Mint Salad	64. Ricotta Cup with Honey and Nuts	67. Pears with Blue Cheese
Lunch	34. Lean Beef Steak with Roasted Vegetables	18. Lentil Soup	18. Lentil Soup
Snack 2	56. Oat and Blueberry Mini Muffins	58. Oat and Dark Chocolate Bars with Hazelnuts	69. Seed Crackers and Chickpea Hummus
Dinner	49. Vegetable and Lentil Soup	48. Baked Cod with Olives and Cherry Tomatoes	38. Eggplant and Chickpea Stew

	Day 22	Day 23	Day 24
Breakfast	10. Breakfast Burrito with Turkey and Avocado	2. Oatmeal, Blueberry, and Cinnamon Muffins	8. Whole Wheat Waffles with Fresh Fruit
Snack 1	66. Banana and Coconuts Ice Cream	70. Mini Chickpea, Vegetable, and Light Basil Pesto Salad	65. Dried Fruit and Seed Mix
Lunch	30. Quinoa and Chickpea Salad	31. Chicken and Vegetable Wrap	22. Mushroom Risotto
Snack 2	70. Mini Chickpea, Vegetable, and Light Basil Pesto Salad	68. Mini Spelt and Banana Pancakes	62. Date and Almond Balls
Dinner	39. Baked Cod with Tomato, Rosemary, and Turmeric	42. Turkey and Vegetable Skillet Ingredients: Quantity for 1 person	43. Stir-Fried Beef and Broccoli

	Day 25	Day 26	Day 27
Breakfast	13. Whole Wheat Crepes with Ricotta and Raspberries	9. Whole Wheat Pancakes with Sugar-Free Maple Syrup	15. Berry and Chia Seed Smoothie Bowl
Snack 1	60. Cinnamon Apple Chips with Dried Fruit and Seeds	68. Mini Spelt and Banana Pancakes	69. Seed Crackers and Chickpea Hummus
Lunch	23. Fish Tacos with Avocado and Red Cabbage	28. Whole Wheat Spaghetti with Tomato and Basil	33. Salmon Burger
Snack 2	67. Pears with Blue Cheese	63. Pineapple and Mint Salad	64. Ricotta Cup with Honey and Nuts
Dinner	47. Steamed Turkey Meatballs with Vegetables	40. Chicken Stuffed with Spinach and Feta	44. Grilled Vegetable Salad with Quinoa

	Day 28	Day 29	Day 30
Breakfast	3. Spinach and Light Feta Frittata	8. Whole Wheat Waffles with Fresh Fruit	8. Whole Wheat Waffles with Fresh Fruit
Snack 1	65. Dried Fruit and Seed Mix	69. Seed Crackers and Chickpea Hummus	62. Date and Almond Balls
Lunch	23. Fish Tacos with Avocado and Red Cabbage	24. Smoked Salmon Salad	25. Vegetable Frittata
Snack 2	60. Cinnamon Apple Chips with Dried Fruit and Seeds	65. Dried Fruit and Seed Mix	58. Oat and Dark Chocolate Bars with Hazelnuts
Dinner	51. Lemon and Thyme Chicken with Steamed Vegetables	54. Spinach and Mushroom Frittata	50. Ratatouille with Polenta

9.2 BONUS 2: Index

(Search for the recipe you want starting from the ingredients you have in the fridge)

9.3   BONUS 3 Weight Loss e BONUS 4 Workout

The book is complete; however, I want to gift you two bonuses, which we'll call Bonus 3 and 4. Scan the QR code and download them.

To my dear grandmother Grace

Printed in Great Britain
by Amazon

43055163R00044